Meditations on Life
~A Year with God~

by
Doctor John Lawrence

Perfected Pen Publishing
www.PerfectedPen.com
www.SabrinaKCarpenter.com
www.PerfectedPenPublishing.com

ISBN-10: 0982773730
ISBN-13: 978-0982773734

Dedication

These meditations are dedicated to the fond memory of my father, Reverend Robert I. Lawrence and to my mother, Nettie Lou Bradley Lawrence.

These meditations are also dedicated to the lives of the men and women who gave their lives for the guidance and benefit of mankind throughout history.

I thank those who gave me encouragement and helped me correct the manuscript.

Thanks to Allyson Carter, Johnny Lawrence, Ginger Burton and my wife, Audie, for helping me and for her patience as I spent many hours away from her as I prepared the manuscript.

Bible verses quoted in this book are from the New American Standard version.
Information of people, times and places are from Wikipedia and the Catholic encyclopedia.

New Year

Scripture

28 Do you not know? Have you not heard? The everlasting God, the Lord, the creator of the ends of the earth does not become weary or tired. His understanding is inscrutable.
29 He gives strength to the weary. And to him who lacks might, He gives power.
30 Though youths become weary and tired, and vigorous men stumble badly.
31 Yet those who wait for the Lord Will grow new strength; they will mount up with wings of eagles, They will run and not get tired, they will walk and not become weak.
Isaiah 40: 28 - 31

17 Therefore, if anyone is in Christ, he is a new creature: The old things passed away but the new things have come.
2 Corinthians 5: 17

3 Jesus answered and said to him, "Truly, truly, I say to you, unless one is born again he cannot see the Kingdom of God."
John 3: 3

Meditation

This is the first week of the New Year. Through the word people celebrate the end of an old year and the beginning of a new year. We have made resolutions that we intend to keep. Some will keep them but a lot will forget about them by the end of the week. Some of us will have hangovers, guilt and suffer from the thing that we did the year before.

This is a good time to resolve not to do the things that we regretted during the year before. Saul of Tarsus was a devout Hebrew that strongly believed that he was doing the correct thing by doing what the church leaders believed. He thought that it was God's will for him to persecute, imprison and stone to death those who had become Christian. One day, on the road to Damascus, God shined a great light in Saul's eyes and blinded him. He was led to Damascus where God sent Ananias to find him

17 So Anaias departed and entered the house, and after laying hands on him and said, "Brother Saul, the Lord Jesus has appeared to you on the road by which you were coming has sent me so that you might regain your sight and be filled by the Holy Spirit."
Acts 9: 17

Saul was converted to a new way of life and was re-named Paul. His spirit was re-bourn and he became a new creature, a devout follower of Christ Jesus and his way of life. We also can become new in spirit. We can learn to be a new person in we learn to live a new life and follow the teachings of Christ. As we start a new year let us think and meditate on the words of Paul that he said to the church in Philipi.

8 "Finally brethren, whatever is true, whatever honorable, whatever is right, whatever is lovely, whatever is in good report, if there is any excellence and anything worthy of praise, dwell on these things.
Philippians 4: 8

Thoughts for the Week

Now let us from this table rise renewed in body, mind, and soul; with Christ we die, and live again. His selfless love has made us whole. With minds alert upheld by grace to spread the Word in speech and deed, we follow in the steps of Christ at one with all in hope and need. To fill each human house with love, it is the Sacrament of care; the work that Christ began to do we humbly pledge ourselves to share.
Then grant us courage, Father God to choose again the pilgrims' way and help us to accept with the challenge of tomorrow's day.
Fred Kaan, 1964

Prayer

Almighty and everlasting father, Gods of all of those before us, we give thanks to you for being with us, Providing for us and guiding us through the years. We pray that you will continue to be with us through your Son, Christ Jesus, as we begin a new year. May we be steadfast in your will and throughout the coming year and through every year of our lives. We pray this in the name of Christ Jesus.
Amen

God's Creation

Scripture

1 In the beginning God created the heavens and the earth.
2 The earth was formless and void, and darkness was upon the surface of the deep.
3 Then God said, "Let there be light", and there was light.
4 God saw the light that it was good, and God separated the light from the darkness.
5 God called the light day, and the darkness the called night. And there was evening there was morning, one day
Genesis 1: 1 -5

11 Then God said, "Let the earth sprout vegetation: plants yielding seed and fruit trees on the earth bearing fruit after their kind with seed in them; and it was so.
Genesis 1: 11

14 Then God said, "Let there be light in the expanse of the heavens to separate the day from the night, and let there be for signs and for seasons and for days and years;
15 and let there be for light for expanse of the heavens to give light on the earth"; and it was so.
Genesis: 1

20 Then God said, "Let the waters team with teams of living creatures; and let birds fly over the earth in the open expanse of the heavens."
Genesis 1: 20

24 Then God said, "Let the earth bring forth living creatures after their kind; Cattle and creeping things and beast of the earth after their kind", and it was so.
Genesis 1: 24

26 Then God said, "Let Us make man in our image according to

our likeness; and let them rule over the fish and over the birds of the sky and over the cattle and over all the earth, and every creeping thing that creeps on the earth.
Genesis 1: 26

Meditation

As I sit on the porch in the mornings meditating on God's magnificent creation I sit in awe at what God has done. As the sun rises over the trees and mountains, new leaves seem to spring forth. The grasses and other plants burst into buds and beautiful flowers. The leaves clean the air after being used by machines, plants, automobiles, animals, and man. The leaves recycle the air, cleaning the air of carbon dioxide and giving off oxygen to be used again.

I think of how God has created the plants and animals of the seas and then the plants and animals that cover the earth. After vegetation, God created animals to roam the earth. They had ample vegetation to eat, grow and reproduce. Hummingbirds, bees and other insects fed on the nectar of the flowers and pollinated the plants so that they could produce seed to propagate themselves.

As I feel the cool breeze and inhale the clean cool air I began to reflect on our bodies. Newborn babies are clean, pure, and fresh form God. I recall the times that I have cut or bruised myself. An army of blood cells came to the defense and began to clean up the injured tissue, contamination and germs. The wound became inflamed and red as the battle progressed. After the inflammation cleared and the wound was clean, millions of worker cells came and repaired the wound, leaving a scar much like the seam after a welder repairs a pipe. When we break a bone, millions of cells clear the blood and injured bone. Other cells come and after a few months the break is repaired. When our bodies are invaded by bacteria, viruses, or fungi, our immune system sends an army of cells to attack and defeat the invading enemy.

When I recall what my God given defenses have done for me, I remember the time when I had a respiratory infection and the doctor took an X-ray, and told me that in the past I had been infected with TB (tuberculosis). He said that my natural defenses had destroyed all the TB germs and all that was left was two healed scars where the battles had been fought. He gave me some cough syrup and said that my own defenses would take care of the rest. A few years ago I stepped into a blood mobile to give blood. A few days later I received a letter stating that my blood could not be used because it had antibodies against Hepatitis C virus. I must have stuck myself with a contaminated needle and my immune system had destroyed the hepatitis C virus. Yes! Yes! We do have an awesome creator.

Thoughts for the Week

This is my Father's world, and to my listening ears all nature sings, and round me rings the music of the spheres. This is my Father's world: I rest me in the thought of rocks and trees, of skies and seas, his hand the wonders wrought.

This is my Father's world, the birds their carols raise, the morning light, the lily white, declare their makers praise. This is my father's world; he shines in all that's fair, in the rustling grass I hear him pass; he speaks to me everywhere.

This is my Father's world; O let me ne'er forget that though the wrong seems oft so strong God is the ruler yet.
This is my Father's world; why should my heart be sad?
The Lord is King; let the heavens ring! God reigns; let the earth be glad.

Maltbie D Babcock, 1901

Prayer

See the morning sun ascending, radiant in the eastern sky; hearing angel's voices blending in their praise to God on high!

So may we in lowly station, join the choristers above;
singing with the whole creation, Praise thee for thy great love.

For the loving kindness ever shed upon our earthly way.
For the mercy, ceasing never for the blessing day by day;
"Wisdom, Honor, Power, and Blessing!" With the angelic host we
cry; round thy throne, thy name confessing, Lord, we would to thee
draw nigh. Alleluia! Alleluia! Glory be to God on high! Amen

Charles Parkin 1952

The Temple of the Soul

Scripture

18 Flee immorality. Every sin that a man commits is outside the body, but the immoral man sins against his own body.
19 Or do you not that your body is a temple of the Holy Spirit who is in you whom you have from God, and that you are not your own.
1 Corinthians 6: 18, 19

22 Then the Lord God said," Behold, the man has become like one of Us, knowing good and evil; and now, he might stretch out his hand, and take from the tree of life, and eat and live forever."----
23 therefore the Lord God sent him out of the garden of Eden, to cultivate the ground, from which he was taken.
Genesis 3: 22, 23

8 The Lord then spoke to Aaron, saying,
9 "Do not drink wine or strong drink, neither you nor your sons with you come into the tent meeting, so
you will not die-----it is a perpetual status throughout your generation----
10 and so as to make a distinction between the body and the profane, and between the unclean and clean.
Leviticus 10: 8 - 10

17 Do not let your heart envy sinners, but live in the fear of the Lord always.
18 Surely there is a future, And your hope will not be cut off.
19 Listen my on, and be wise, and direct your heart in the way.
20 Do not be with heavy drinkers of wine or with gluttonous eaters of meats,
21 For the heavy drinker and glutton will come to Poverty, And drowsiness will cloth one with rags
Proverbs 23: 17 - 21

Meditation

Our bodies are the temples of our souls. It has been said that the mind is between the spirit and the soul. Our minds may be filled with the Holy Spirit, the spirit of truth and love, or the spirit of the Devil, the spirit of hatred and lies. Our bodies are what caries our spirit, mind and soul around into this world. The health of our bodies depends on how we treat it. Through the bible, God has given us suggestions for keeping our bodies in good health.

When man chose to gain knowledge of good and evil and be like God, God drove man out of the Garden of Eden. Man, then had to work to provide food, clothing and shelter for himself. Medical science knows that the body needs to move and work in order for the muscles to remain strong and for the joints not to become stiff. It is a pleasure to taste, see and feel what our work has done.

God also instructed us not to be drunk with hard drink and wine. Alcohol does lower inhibitions and people can be able to be more sociable and less inhibited. A little more alcohol in the brain allows a person to be less inhibited and their real feelings come forth. Some will become happy and become more sociable. Others will become more loving. Others will become sad and sorry for the things that they have or have not done and even begin to cry. Others will become angry, hateful and want to fight. Prolonged use can destroy some of the brain and the temple of the soul. Other mind and body altering drugs are used as our social life develops and as we are influenced by others. These drugs are addicting and habit forming. Smoking tobacco destroys the lungs and many people have difficulty breathing, working, thinking, and the body dies early. Other social drugs destroy the mind and temple of the soul.

God intended for man's body to remain healthy and have a long life. Life is much better if a man and a woman love each other, marry and raise a happy, healthy family. Lust leads many people to commit adultery and other abnormal sexual practices. This behavior leads to sexually transmitted diseases such as Syphilis, which causes brain and spinal cord injury, HIV or AIDS which destroys the immune system and other diseases such as gonorrhea, herpes and cervical cancer destroy the temple of the soul.

Thoughts for the Week

Be still my soul, and know the Lord is on your side.
Bear patiently the cross of grief or pain;
leave to your God to order and provide;
in every change God's faithful will remain.
Be still, my soul: your best, you're heavenly
through thorny ways lead to a joyful end.

Be still my soul: Your God will undertake
to guide the future, as in ages past.
Your hope, your confidence let nothing shake;
all now mysterious shall be bright at last.
Be still, my soul; the waves and wind still know
the Christ who ruled them while he dwelt below.

Be still, my soul: the hour is hastening on
when we will be forever with the Lord,
when disappointments , grief and fears are gone,
Sorrow forgot, love's purest joys restored.
Be still, my soul; when change and tears are past,
and safe and blessed we shall meet at last.

Katharina Von Sledge, 1752

Prayer

Spirit of God, descend upon my heart;
wean it from earth; through all pulses move;
stoop to my weakness, mighty as thou art,
and make me love thee as I ought to love.

I ask no dream or prophetic ecstasies 1

no sudden rendering of the veil of clay,
no angel visitant, no opening skies;
but take the dimness of my soul away.

Have thou not bid me love thee, Lord and King?
All, all thine own sol, heart, and strength and mind.
I see thy cross; there teach my heart to cling.
O let me seek thee, and O let me find!

Teach me to feel that thou art always nigh;
teach me the struggles of the soul to bear.
to check the rising doubt, the rebel sigh,
teach me the patience of unanswered prayer.

Teach me to love thee as thine angels love,
And holy passion filling all my frame;
The kindling of the heavenly descended Dove,
My heaven and altar and thy love the flame.

George Croly, 1867

Martin Luther King Day

Scripture

25 And a lawyer stood up and put Him to the test, saying, "Teacher, what shall I do to inherit eternal life?"
26 And He said to him, 'What is written in the law? How does it read to you?"
27 And he answered, "YOU SHALL LOVE THE LORD YOUR HEART, AND WITH ALL YOUR SOUL, AND WITH ALL YOUR STRENGTH, AND WITH ALL YOUR MIND, AND YOUR NEIGHBOR AS YOURSELF.
28 And He said to him, 'You have answered correctly. Do this and you will live."
29 But wishing to justify himself, he said to Jesus, "And who is my neighbor?
30 Jesus replied and said, A man was going down from Jerusalem to Jericho, and fell among robbers, and they striped him and beat him, and went away leaving him dead.
31 And by chance a priest was going down on that road and when he saw him, he passed by on the other side,
32 "Likewise, a Levite also, when he came to the place and saw him, passed by on the other side.
33 "But a Samaritan who was on a journey, came upon him; and when he say him he felt compassion.
34 and came to him and bandaged up his wounds, pouring oil and wine on them and he put him on his own beast, and brought him to an inn and took care of him.
35 "On the next day he took out two danari and gave them to the innkeeper and gave them to the innkeeper and said, "take care of him and whatever more you spend, when I return I will repay.
36 "Which of these three proved to be a neighbor to the man who fell into the robber' hands?"
37And he said, "Those who showed mercy toward him. Then Jesus said to him, "Go and do likewise.
Luke 10: 25 -37

43 "You have heard that it was said "You should love your love neighbor and hate your enemy.

44 "But I say to you, love your enemy and pray for those who persecute you

45 so that you may be sons of your Father who is in heaven; for He causes the sun to rise on the evil and good, and sends rain on the righteous and on the unrighteous.

46 "for if you love those who love you, what reward do you have? Do not even the tax collectors do the same?

47 "If you greet only your brother, what more do you do that others? Do not even the Gentiles do the same?

48 "Therefore you are to be perfect, as your heavenly father is perfect."

Matthew 5: 43 -48

Meditation

On January 15, 1925, a man named Martin Luther King Jr. was born. After graduating from Morehouse College in Atlanta, Georgia, he studied theology at Crozer Theological Seminary in Pennsylvania. He was elected president of a predominantly white senior class and was awarded a B.D. degree in 1951. He earned a doctorate from Boston University in 1955.

As president of the Southern Christian Leadership Conference, Doctor King patterned the operational techniques of non-violence and soul force, after Mahatma Gandhi. Under his leadership the Afro-American experienced less of the injustice, prejudices, and segregation practices through the non-violent and soul force means than they had ever before experienced in America.

When Martin Luther King Jr. was awarded the Nobel Peace Prize, he stated that he would rather be known for what he had done for the brotherhood of man than as the winner of the coveted Nobel Peace Prize. In his historic speech, "I have a Dream," he said, "Now is the time to lift our nation out of the quicksand of racial injustice to the solid rock of brotherhood. Now is the time to make justice a reality to all of God's children. I have a dream that one day this nation will rise up and live out the true meaning of its creed: "We hold these truths to be self-evident, that all men are created equal...I have a dream that on the red hills of Georgia, the sons of former slaves and the sons of former slave owners will be able to sit down together at the table of brotherhood...I have a dream that for my little children will one day live in a nation where they will not be judged by the color of their skin but by the content of their character."

Thoughts for the Week

In God there is no east or west, in Him no south or north; but one great fellowship
of love thought the whole wide earth.

In Christ shall true hearts everywhere their high communion find; his service is the
golden cord close binding all human kind.

In Christ now meets both east and west in Him meet south and north; all Christly souls
one in him through the whole wide world.

Prayer

Our gracious heavenly Father, creator of all mankind, we praise your holy name.
We give thanks to You for souls such as Martin Luther King Jr.
May we live in harmony with all of Your children as well as all of Your creation.
May we see others for the content of their character rather that their race, religion or creed.
Amen

Man

Scripture

26 Then God said, "let us make man in our image, according to our likeness and let them rule over the fish of the sea and over the birds of the sky; and over the cattle and over all the earth, and over every creeping thing that creeps on the earth.
27 God created man in His image; the image of God He created him; male and female He created them.
28 "Be fruitful and multiply, and fill the earth and subdue it; and rule over the fish of the sea and the birds of the sky; and every living thing that moves on the earth".
Genesis 1: 26 -28

7 Then the Lord God formed man out of the dust of the ground, and breathed into his nostril the breath of life, and man became a living thing.
Genesis 2: 7

1 Now the serpent was more crafty than any beast of the field which the Lord God had made. And he said to the woman, "Indeed, has God said, "You shall not eat from any tree in the garden?"
2 The woman said to the serpent, "From the fruit of the trees of the garden we may eat.
3 But from the fruit of the tree in which is in the middle, God has said, "You may not eat from it or touch it, or you will die."
4 The serpent said to the woman, "You surely will not die."
5 "For God knows that from the day you eat from it your eyes will be opened , and you will be like God, knowing good and evil."
Genesis 3: 1-5

Meditation

Notice that in Genesis 1: 26 God said, "Let us create man in our image; according to our likeness." Then in Genesis 2: 7 the bible reads, "Then the Lord God formed man of the dust of the ground, and breathed into his nostril the breath on life, and man became a living being. Our physical bodies were made from the dust of the ground and breath, eat, walk, run, and reproduce like the loser animals. A perfect body it is. Then God created the mind and soul of man in His own image. He said, "Let us make man in "Our image." As we grow, learn grow in mind, spirit, truth and love we have the ability to love, hate, think and know right from wrong. God came to earth in the human body of Jesus and is the Christ that showed us how to love and live in harmony with our fellow man. That mind and soul, created through the spirit of God, is what separates us from the lower animals. The soul is what will live in the warmth of god's love when we pass to the nest life. I have heard it said that the mind is between the spirit and the soul. God is love and God is truth.
7 Beloved, let us love one another, for love is from God; and everyone who is born of God; and everyone who loves is born of God and is of God and knows God.
8 The one who does not know love does not know God; for God is love.
9 By this the love of God was manifested in us that God has sent his only begotten Son into the world that we might live through Him. 1 John 4: 7 -9

God, our creator, is the great spirit of truth, love, and light, the power behind all creation. This we can believe but may not fully understand. As Paul told us, we understand only in part and see God as though looking through smoky glass. We will not fully know our creator until we see Him face-to-face.

Thoughts for the Week

God created heaven and earth, all things perfect brought to birth,
God's great power made dark and light, Earth revolves day and
night.

Let us praise God's mercy great; and our needs that love await,
God who fashions all that lives to each one a blessing gives.

God is one, will ever be; handmade idols of vanity; handmade gods
of wood and clay cannot help us when we pray Gut God's grace
beyond compare save us all from Earth's despair so earth's
creatures Small and great give thanks for the blessed state.
Trad Tiawanese hymn; translated by Clare Anderson, 1983
(Genesis 1: 1 -5)

Prayer

Spirit of the living God, fall afresh on me, Spirit of the living God,
and fall afresh on me.
Melt me, mold me, fill me, and use me. Spirit of the living God,
fall afresh on me.
Daniel Iverson, 1926 (Acts 11: 15)

Almighty, omnipotent, ever-present, and everlasting God, maker of
mankind, guide us as we strive to develop our minds and souls
more like you. May we always be mindful of what you are and
what you taught us while you walked the earth in the body of Jesus
the Christ. May we meditate on your will, love, and truth as we try
to walk in your steps.
Amen

God's Word

Scripture

1 Then God spoke all these words, saying
2 "I am the Lord your God, who bought you out of the land of Egypt, out of the house of slavery.
3 "You shall have no other God before me.
4 'You shall not make for yourselves any idols of any likeness of what is in the heaven above the earth or on the earth beneath or in the waters beneath the earth.
5 "You may not worship them, or serve them: for the Lord your God, am a jealous God, visiting the iniquity of the fathers or the children, on the third and the forth generation of those who hate me.
6 but showing loving kindness to thousands to those who love Me and keep My commandments.
7 "You shall not take the name of the Lord your God in vain, for the Lord will not leave him unpunished who take His name in vain.
8 "Remember the Sabbath Day, to keep it holy.
9 "Six days you shall labor and do all your work.
10 "but the seventh day is a Sabbath of the Lord your God; in it you shall not do any work. Your sons and daughters, your male and your female servants or your cattle or your sojourner who stay with you.
11 "For in six days the Lord made the heavens and the earth, the sea and all that is in them, and rested on the seventh day; therefore the Lord blessed the Sabbath day and made it holy.
12 "Honor your father and you mother, that your days may be prolonged in the land which the lore your God gave you.
13 "You shall not murder.
14 "Your shall not commit adultery.
15 "You shall not steal.
16 "You shall not bear false witness against your neighbor.
17 "You shall not covet your neighbor's house; you shall not covet your neighbor's wife or his male servant or his female servant or his ox or his donkey or things that belong to your neighbor.
Exodus 20: 1 - 17

1 Now when the people saw that Moses delayed to coming down from the mountain, the people assembled before Aaron and said to him, "Come, make us a god who will go before us; as for this Moses, this man who brought us up from the land of Egypt, we do not know what has become of him.
Exodus 32: 1

7 The Lord spoke to Moses, "Go down at once, for the people, who you brought from the land of Egypt, have corrupted themselves.
8 "They have quickly turned aside from the way I commanded them. They have made for themselves a golden calf, and have worshiped it and have sacrificed to it and have said, "This is your god, Oh Israel, who brought you
up from the land of Egypt.
9 The Lord said to Moses, "I have seen the people and, and behold, they are an obstinate people.
Exodus 37: 7 -9

19 It came about, as soon as Moses came near the camp that he says the calf and the dancing; and Moses' anger burned and he threw the tablets from his hand and shattered them at the foot of the mountain.
20 He took the calf which they had made and burned it with fire and ground it to powder, and scattered it over the surface of the water and made the sons of Israel drink it...
21 Then Moses said to Aaron, "What did the people do to you that made you have brought such grave sin upon them?"
22 Aaron said "Let not the anger of my Lord burn, you know the people yourself, that they are prone to evil.
Exodus 32: 19 -22

Meditations

God had spoken to Moses, saying, "I am the Lord your God, who brought you out of the land of Egypt, out of the house of slavery. You shall have no other gods before Me. You shall not make for yourselves and idol or any likeness of what is in heaven above or on the earth beneath or in the water under the earth. You shall not worship them or serve them for on the children, of the third and the fourth generation of those who hate Me, but showing loving kindness to those who love Me and keep My commandments Exodus 20: 1 -5

The early Israelites had been through a lot since being taken into captivity by the Egyptians. Their main concern was what God would do for them. They had trusted God and Moses to lead them out of captivity. After wandering in the wilderness, facing starvation and thirst they lost faith in God and Moses and made a golden image as a god to lad them.

As children, we are taught to believe in God and trust in Him. As we grow older we begin to desire and worship material things, such as money, gold, and other things that we feel, see, and can touch. Some even acquire material things through greed, deception, and force, even theft, deception, or murder. Some worship themselves and the things that they have done or acquired, by whatever means and become self-righteous. They do not know or have forgotten that God said that it is better to store up treasures in heaven rather than on earth where they are destroyed by decay and rust and where thieves break in and steal. However, some of us remain true to our teachings, God's word, and acquire self-respect and peace. It is a better, more satisfying, and rewarding life to live by God's words of faith, justice, mercy, and love than to suffer the fear, anxiety, and guilt of selfishness and greed.

Jesus taught us in the parable of the sower that some will hear the word of God but will turn a deaf ear and fall by the wayside. Some will hear the word of God, believe it for a little while but their belief will be like seed that falls on stony ground and will not take roots, whither and die. Some will listen to the word of God, live by it for a little while, but the thorns and weeds, and sins of greed, pride, and self-righteousness will choke out the memory of the word of God. Some will hear the word of God, believe in it and their belief will be like the seed that fall on fertile ground and grow in everlasting trust and love of God. These will live their lives in the kingdom of God and live forever in the warmth of God's love.

Thoughts for the Week

Where we walk with the Lord in the light of his word, what glory he sheds on our way!
When we do his good will, he abides with us still, and with all who will trust and obey.

Not a burden we bear, not a sorrow we share. But our toil he doth richly repay.
Not a grief nor a loss, not a frown or a cross, but is blessed in we trust and obey.

But we never can prove the delights of his love, until all on the alter we lay;
For the favor he shows, for the joy he bestows, never fear, only trust and obey.

Then in fellowship sweet we will sit at his feet, or we'll walk by his side in the way;
What he says we will do, where he sends we will go; never fear, only trust and obey.
John Sammis, 1887

Prayer

Almighty and everlasting Lord, God of truth and God of love, we worship and praise thy Holy Name. We hear your word. May we always abide by your word and never let the weeds and thorns of sin and doubt choke out what we have heard and learned what you have said. Amen

Faith and Trust

Scripture

1 Shout joyfully to the Lord, all the earth.
2 Serve the Lord with gladness; Come before Him with joyful singing.
3 Know that the Lord Himself is God; it is He who has made us, and not we ourselves; we are His people and the sheep of His pasture.
4 Enter His gates with thanksgiving and His courts with praise. Give thanks, and bless His name.
5 The Lord is good; His loving kindness is everlasting and His faithfulness to all generations.
Psalms 100: 1 -5

1 Do not let your heart be troubled; believe in God, believe also in Me.
2 "In My Father's house there are many dwelling places; if it were not so, I would have told you,; for I go to prepare a place for you.
3 "If I go and prepare a place for you, I will come again and receive you to Myself, that where I am you might be also.
4 And you know the way where I am going.
5 Thomas said to Him, "Lord, we do not know where You are going, how do we know the way?"
6 Jesus said to him, "I am the way, the truth, and the light; no one comes to the Father but through Me.
John 14: 1 - 6

3 Blessed be the God and father of our Lord, Jesus Christ, who according to His great mercy has caused us to be born again a living hope through the resurrection of Jesus Christ from the dead,
4 to obtain an inheritance which is imperishable and undefiled and will not fade away, reserved in heaven for you.
5 who are protected by the power of God through fain in salvation ready to be revealed in the last time.
1 Peter 1: 2 - 5

Meditation

David was the youngest of eight sons born to Jesse. He was a shepherd boy. He faced dangers each day while tending the sheep. He wrote psalms of his faith and trust in God, his Lord. He attributed his strength and ability to defend his sheep and himself to the Lord. Many of his psalms like, "The Lord is my shepherd", we read and memorize for strength and encouragement. His faith and trust led him to find favor in the Lord.

When King Saul became disobedient to God, the people of Israel decided to find a new king. The people came to Samuel, who had judged Israel since he was a young man and who had found Saul and anointed him as king of Israel. Before the death of Saul, with his faith in God, David had the courage to go before the Philistine giant, Goliath, and defeat him with his shepherds' sling. The people of Israel turned to David as the leader of Israel and sang songs proclaiming him as king of Israel.

Saul became jealous of David and planned to kill him on several occasions. David continued to defend Israel and had chances to kill Saul, but did not choose to do so. Because of his steadfast faith and trust in God, David became king of Israel, after the death of Saul.

As Simon Peter said, "We have faith that through the life of Jesus Christ, the love of God will sustain us throughout all our life if we place our trust in Him." We can be reassured that our trust in Him will carry us through our troubles and temptations until we are in His loving care through eternity.

Thoughts for the Week

If thou but suffer God to guide thee, and hope in God through all thy ways,
God will give strength, what e'er betide thee and bear thee through evil days,
 which trust in God's unchanging love built of the rock that naught can move.
Only be still, and wait God's leisure in cheerful hope, with heart content to take
what e'er the Maker's pleasure and all discerning love hath sent; we know our inmost wants are known, for we are called to be God's own.

Sing, pray and keep God's way unswerving; so thine faithfully, and trust God's word;
through undeserving; thou yet shall find it true for thee.
 God never yet for soul at need the soul that trusted God indeed.
George Neumark, 1657

Prayer

Dear Lord and father of mankind, for forgive our foolish ways, re-clothe us in our
rightful mind, in purer lives thy service find, in deeper reverence, praise.

In simple trust like those who heard, beside the Syrian sea, the gracious calling
of the Lord, let us, like them, without a word, rise up and follow thee.
John Greenleaf Whittier, 1872
Amen

Abraham Lincoln's Birthday

Scripture

1 Behold, how good and how pleasant it is for brothers to dwell in unity!
2 It is like the precious oil upon the head coming down the beard, even Aaron's beard coming down upon the edge of the robe.
3 It is like the dew or Hermon coming down the mountain of Zion; For the Lord commands the blessing-Life
Forever.
Psalms 13: 1 -3

31 So Jesus was saying to the Jews who had believed Him, "If you continue in My word, then you are true disciples of Mine
32 and you will know the truth, and the truth will make you free.
33 They answered Him, "We are Abraham's descendants and have never yet been enslaved to anyone; how is it that You say, 'You will become free?"
34 Jesus answered, "Truly, truly, I say to you everyone who commits sin is a slave to sin.
35 "The slave does not remain in the house forever, the son does remain forever.
36 "So if the son makes you free, you will be free indeed."
John 8: 31 - 36

16 Act as free men, and do not use your freedom as covering for evil, but use it as bond slaves of God.
17 Honor all people, love the brotherhood, fear God, and honor the King."
Peter 2: 16, 17

Meditation

Abraham Lincoln, in his Gettysburg Address stated, "Four score and seven years ago forefathers brought forth, upon this continent a new nation, conceived in liberty and dedicated to the proposition that all men are created equal."

Abraham Lincoln was born in a log cabin in Kentucky, February 12, 1809. His parents, Thomas and Nancy Lincoln, were uneducated, illiterate farmers, although they were prominent citizens. They belonged to the Baptist church that pulled away from a larger church because they refused to support slavery. Abe Lincoln was exposed to anti-slavery sentiments at a very young age.

Abraham Lincoln's formal education was about eight months by a traveling teacher. He was in effect self-educated, studying every book that he could borrow. He mastered the bible, English History, and American History. He studied law and was admitted to the Illinois bar at the age of twenty-six. That was the first year he made his first protest against slavery in the Illinois House of Representatives.

During the Civil War, reconstruction of the union weighed heavily on President Lincoln's mind. "Let 'em up easy" he told General Ulysses S Grant. Because of his determined effort and love for freedom, Abraham Lincoln succeeded in abolishing slavery and healing the union. The brotherhood of man in America was preserved.

Abraham found his life by giving it all for what he believed and for freedom and brotherhood. He is not the only one who has molded the course of history and making the world a better place for all of us to live in love and harmony. We also can live a joyful and fulfilling life by giving ourselves for others.

Thoughts for the Week

Let my people seek the freedom in the wilderness a while slave pens of the
Delta, from the ghettos of the Nile":
For God spoke from out of Sinai, for God spoke and it was done, and the people crossed the
Water to the rising of the sun.

"Let the people seek their freedom in the wilderness a while, from the ageing shrines and structure, from the cloister and the isle." So the son of God has spoken, and the storm clouds are unfurled, for God's people must be scattered to be servants in the world.

When we murmur on the mountains for the old Egyptian plans, when we miss out accent
bondage, and the hope, the promise waters; the rock shall yield its water and the manna
fall by night and with visions of a future shall we march to-ward the light,

In the maelstrom of the nation, in journeying into space, in the clash of generation, in the hungering for grace, in our agony and glory we call to newer ways by the Lord of our
tomorrows and to the God of earth' today
T. Herbert O'Driscoll, 1971

Prayer

Gracious God,
Make me sensitive to the evidence of your goodness
and may I, trusting you, free myself of the horrors of death,
and feel free to live intensely and happy the life you have given me. Amen
Ruben Alves, Brazil, 20th cent.

Valentine's Day

Scripture

4 And he answered him and said, "Have you not read that He who created them from the beginning MADE THEM MALE AND FEMALE,
5 and said, "for this reason he shall leave his Father and mother and be joined the his wife, and the two
Shall become one flesh"?
6 So they are no longer two, but one flesh, what Therefore God has joined together, let mo man separate."
Matthew 19 :, 4 - 6

Meditation

Every February has been known as the month of romance around the world, Valentine's Day is celebrated. Cards, candy, flowers, and other gifts are exchanged between loved ones as an expression of love and affection for each other. It was a common belief in France and England that February 14th was the beginning of spring; the time of purification. This added to the thought that Valentine's Day should be a day of romance and fertility.

Valentine is believed to be a priest who served during the third century in France. Emperor Claudius II decided that single men made better soldiers that those with wives of families. For that reason he outlawed marriage of young men. Valentine realized the injustice of this decree and defied the emperor by continuing to perform marriages for young lovers in secret. The emperor discovered Valentine's action and ordered that he be put to death.

According to the legend, Valentine fell in love with a young woman who visited him in prison and was believed to have been the jailer's daughter. Before his death, he wrote her cards and letters and signed them, "from your Valentine." This expression of affection and romance has continued until this day through the exchange of cards, letters and gifts. During the middle ages, Saint Valentine was one of the most popular saints in France and England.

Thoughts for the Week

Where love is found and hope comes home, Sing and be glad that two are one,
Praise God and share our Maker's joy,
When love has flowered in trust and care build each day the love that may dare
to reach beyond homes warmth and light to serve and strive for truth and right

Where love is tried and loved ones change, hold still to hope through senses strange,
till ease returns, and love grows wise through listening ears and open eyes.

When love is torn and trust betrayed Pray strength to love till torrents fades,
Lovers keep no score of wrong, But bear through pain love's Easter song.

Praise God for love, praise God for life, In age of youth, husband, wife.
Lift up your hearts, let love be fed
through death and life in broken bread.
Brian Wren, 1978

Prayer

Almighty and ever loving heavenly Father, You have so consecrated the covenant of Christian marriage that in it represents the covenant between Christ and His church. Send therefore, Your blessing upon these two, that they may keep their marriage covenant and so grow in love and godliness together that their

homes might be a haven of blessing and Peace through Jesus Christ our Lord.
Amen

President's Day

Scripture

10 "Therefore, come now, and I will show you to Pharaoh, so that you may bring My people, the sons of Israel, out of Egypt.
11 But Moses said to God, "Who am I that I should go to Pharaoh and that I should bring the sons of Israel out of Egypt?"
12 And He said, "Certainly I will be with you and shall be the sign to you that it is I who have sent you, when you have brought the people out of Egypt, you shall worship God in the mountains,
Exodus 3: 10 - 12

19 "Show me the coins used for pole tax." And they brought to Him a denarius.
20 And He said to them, "Whose likeness and inscription is this?"
21 They said to Him, "Caesar's," Then He said to them, "Then render to
22 Caesar the things that are Caesar's and to God the things that are Gods.
Matthew 22: 19 - 21

25 And He said to them, "The King of the Gentiles lord it over them, and those who have authority over them are called "benefactors",
26 "But it is not the way with you, but the one who is the greatest among you must become like your youngest, and leader like the servant.
27 "For who is greater, those who recline at the table or the one who Serves? Is it not the one who reclines at the table? But I am among you as the one who serves.
Matthew 22: 25 - 27

Meditation

In England in the late sixteenth century everyone was forced to belong to a church controlled by the King who was in power.

Those who dared to publicly express or teach different beliefs were imprisoned or hanged. William Brewster, William Bradford, and a group of pilgrims who desired religious freedom sailed for America and formed the Plymouth colony in New England. By the grace of God and the help of some friendly Indians, the pilgrims made it through the rough first winter and began to grow in number during the spring and summer.

The people had freedom to worship as they pleased but the English government continued to control a lot of their lives, government and trade. Under the leadership of the first American President, General George Washington, and others, the thirteen colonies, fought and won their independence from English domination.

The thirteen colonies formed a representative government and constitution of the United States of America. They developed and wrote a declaration of independence. The united declaration of the United States of America declared their beliefs and laws:

When in the course of human events it becomes necessary for one people to dissolve the political bonds which have connected them with another and to assure among the powers of the earth, the separate and equal stations to which the laws of nature and the nature's God entitles them, a decent respect to the Opinion of Mankind requires that they should declare the causes which impel them to the separation.

We hold these truths to be self-evident. That all men are created equal, that they are endowed by the Creator which contain inalienable Rights; that among these are the Life, Liberty and the pursuit of happiness.

Under the constitution, we in America have enjoyed the freedom to worship as we wish, freedom of speech, and freedom to raise our families as we believe we should. When President Franklin D. Roosevelt was in office the world was threatened by the fascist philosophy. Under the leadership of President Roosevelt, and our allies, fascism was defeated. As fascism was defeated, atheistic communism divided Europe and threatened world peace. Under the leadership of President Ronald Reagan, a lot of communist governments were dissolved or have become more tolerant of freedom.

When President George Bush was president, the western world and most religions were again threatened by terrorist groups. It continues today that our nation, under the leadership of our presidents must guard against threats of terrorism and other ideologies.

We owe our gratitude to our presidents, as well as other elected leaders for helping us remain safe and remain steadfast in our beliefs in God and our pursuit of liberty and happiness.

Thoughts for the Week

A mighty fortress is our God, a bulwark never failing.
Our helper he amid the flood of mortal ills prevailing.
For still our ancient foe doth seek to work us woe; his craft and power are great, and armed with cruel hate, on earth there is no equal.

Did we in our strength confide, our striving would be losing?
Were the right men on our side, the man of God's own choosing?
Dost ask who that might be? Christ Jesus it is he, Lord Sabbath, his name from age to age the same, and we must win the battle.

And though this world, with devils filled, should threaten to undo us,
We will not fear, for God with his truth to triumph through us,
The Prince of Darkness grim, we trouble not for him, his rage we each endure, for lo, his doom is sure, one little word shall fell him.

For were above all earthly powers, no thanks to them abiding.
The spirit and the gifts are ours thru him with us sideth.
Let good and kindred go, the mortal life also, the body
the may kill, God's truth abideth still. His kingdom is forever.
Martin Luther, 1529

Prayer

Dear God and Father of mankind we are eternally grateful for leaders who give themselves to serve the people and guide them in their quest for freedom and safety. May we be thankful for their willingness to serve.
Amen

Saint Patrick's Day

Scripture

9 "I am the door, if anyone enters through me he will be saved, and will go in and out and find pasture,
10 The thief comes only to kill and to steal and to destroy; I come that they may have life and have it more abundantly.
11 "I am the good shepherd; the good shepherd lays down His life for the sheep.
John 10: 9 - 11

1 Hear a just cause, O Lord, give heed to my cry; Give ear to my prayer, which is not from deceitful lips.
2 May my judgment come forth from your presence; Let your eyes look with equity.
3 You have tried my heart; You have visited me by night; You have tested me and You found nothing;
I have purposed that my mouth will not transgress.
Psalm 17: 1 -3

21 But now apart from the law the righteousness of God has been manifested, being witness by the law and the
prophets,
22 even the righteousness of God through faith in Jesus Christ for all those who believe; for there is no distinction;
23 for all have sinned and fall short of the glory of God,
24 being justified by His grace through the redemption which is in Christ Jesus;
25 who God displayed publicly as propitiation in His blood through faith. This was to demonstrate His
righteousness for in the forbearance of God He passed over the sins previously committed.
Romans 3: 21 - 25

Meditation

Saint Patrick was born in Kilpatrick, Scotland in the year 397 and died between 360 and 490 AD. When he was sixteen years old, he was captured by raiders and sold into slavery in Ireland. As his master was a Druid high priest, Patrick became familiar with all the details of Druidism and the Irish speech. He tended his master's flock in the valley of Bfraid and the slopes of Splemish.

Saint Patrick stated in his "confessions" that during his captivity while tending the flock, he prayed may times a day: "the love of God." He added, "and his fear increased in me more and more, and the faith grew in me, and the spirit was roused, so that, in a single day I prayed as many as a hundred prayers, and in the nightly nearly the same, so that while in the wood and the mountain, even before the dawn, I was roused to prayer and felt no hurt from it, whether there was snow or ice or rain nor was there any slothfulness in me.

After six years of captivity and with the influence of an angel, he fled and walked 200 miles until he came to a bay and caught a sailing ship to Brittan. His heart was now seeking to devote himself to the sacred ministry, the Catholic Church. He entered Saint Martin's monastery.

After several years, he became a priest and returned to Ireland. He entered Ireland where the druids were up in arms against him. He continued further where a number of natives heard in their own tongue glad tidings of redemption. Until his death, Saint Patrick preached the story of redemption and the love for life, and with God's help, helped to establish the Catholic Church in Ireland.

Christians and non-Christian people around the world celebrate Saint Patrick's Day and enjoy the love for life. Christians during lent celebrate Saint Patrick's life and the story of Christ's redemption for us.

Thoughts for the Week

Out or the deep have I called unto thee, O Lord; Lord, hear my
voice
Oh let thine ear consider well the voice of my complaint.
If thou, Lord, will be extreme to mark what is done amiss,

O, Lord, who may abide it
For there is mercy with thee; therefore thou shalt be feared.
I look for the Lord; my soul doth wait for him; in his word is my
trust.
My soul fleeth unto thee Lord before the morning watch;

I say before the morning watch,
O Israel, trust in the Lord,
For with God there is mercy, and with him there is plenteous
redemption.
And he shall redeem Israel from all his sins.
Psalm 139

Prayer

Out of the depths I cry t you, O Lord, now hear my calling.
Incline your ear to my distress in spite of my rebelling.
Do not regard my sinful deeds. Sene me the grace my
Sinful needs; without it I am nothing.

My soul is waiting for the Lord, as one who longs for morning;
no watcher watches with greater hope than I for Christ's returning.
I hope as Israel in the Lord, who sends redemption through the
word.
Praise God for endless Mercy. Amen
Martin Luther, 1524

Lent

Scripture

1 Then Jesus was led up by the spirit into the wilderness to be tempted by the devil

2 and after He had fasted for forty days and forty nights, He then became hungry.

3 and the tempter came to him and said, "If you are the Son of God, command these stones to become bread."

4 But He answered him and said, "Man shall not live by bread alone, but on every word that proceeds out of the mouth of God."

5 Then the devil took Him into the holy city and had Him stand on the pinnacle of the temple,

6 and said to Him, "If you are the Son of God, throw Yourself down; for it is written, "He will command His angels concerning You" and, "On their hands they will bear You up, so that You will not strike Your foot against a stone."

7 Jesus said to him, "On the other hand, it is written, "You shall not put the Lord your God to the test."

8 Again the devil took Him to a very high mountain and showed Him all the kingdoms of the world and their glory

9 and said to Him, "All these things I will give you, if You fall down and worship me."

10 Then Jesus said to him, "Go Satan. For it is written, You shall worship the Lord, your God, and serve Him only"

11 Then the devil left Him; and behold angels came and began to minister to him.

Matthew 4: 1 - 11

14 Therefore, since we have a high priest, who has passed through the heaven, Jesus the Son of God, let us hold fast to our confessions.

15 For we do not have a high priest who cannot sympathize with our weakness, but one who has been tempted in all things as we are, yet without sin.

16 Therefore let us draw near with the confidence of grace, so that we may receive mercy and find grace in the time of Need.

Hebrews 4: 14 - 16

5 Stop depriving one another, except for agreement for a time, so that you devote yourselves to prayer, and come together again so that Satan will not temp you because of yourself control.
I Corinthians 7: 5

Meditation

Lent begins forty days before Easter. Easter Sunday is the day we Christians celebrate the resurrection of Jesus. Lent is observed the forty days before Easter Sunday.

Lent in old English is the word for spring.
In many language,s Lent is derived from the Latin word meaning "forty days." Forty is the traditional number of days of discipline, devotional, and preparation. Jesus was in the wilderness forty days praying and fasting in preparation for the beginning of His ministry.

Ash Wednesday is the first day of Lent. Its name came from an ancient practice of placing ashes on the forehead of worshipers as a sign of humility before God, of morning, of sorrow, of death that sin brings into the world.

Today, Lent is marked by a time of prayer and preparation to celebrate Easter.
Jesus fasted for forty days and nights.
Some Christians still fast for some days during Lent to practice self-purification.

As we approach Easter let us prepare our minds and hearts to repent of our misdeeds and of any wrongs to others as we enter the time of repentance and to live a purer life through the redemption of God through the life and rebirth of Christ Jesus.

Thoughts for the Week

Your face Lord, do I seek, Hide not yourself from me.
Seek the Lord, who now is present, call upon the Lord who is near,
Let the wicked forsake their way, and the righteous their thoughts;
let them return, that the Lord may have mercy on them; that our
God may abundantly pardon.

For my thoughts are not your thoughts, neither are Your ways my
ways, saith the Lord.
for as the heavens higher than the earth,so are my ways higher than
your ways
and my thoughts than your thoughts

For the rain and snow come down from heaven, and return not but
water the earth,
may it bring forth and sprout, giving seed to the sower and bread to
the eater,
so that my word that goes out of my mouth; it shall not return to
me empty,
but it shall accomplish that which I intend, and power in the things
for which I sent it.
Isaiah 55: 6 - 11

Prayer

Merciful God
You sent your messenger the prophets
To preach repentance and prepare our way for salvation.
Give us grace to heed your warnings and forsake our ways,
That we may celebrate aright the commemoration of the nativity,
And may await with joy the coming of Christ our redeemer;
Who lives and reigns You and the Holy Spirit,
One God forever and forever, Amen
Laurence Hull Stooker

Ash Wednesday

Scripture

1 Beware of practicing your righteousness before men to be noticed by them; otherwise you have no reward with your father who is in heaven.

2 "So when you give to the poor, do not sound a trumpet before you as the hypocrites do in the synagogues and in the street so that you may be honored by men. Truly I say to you, they have their reward in full.

3 "But when you give to the poor, do not let your left hand know what your right hand is doing.

4 So your giving will be in secret,; and your father who sees what is done in secret will reward you.

5 When you pray do not be as the hypocrites, For they love to stand and pray in the synagogues and on the street corners so that they may be seen by men, "Truly I say to you, they have their reward in full.

6 "But when you pray, go into your inner room, close the door and pray to your father who is in secret, and your father who sees what is done in secret will reward you.

7 "And when you are praying, do not use meaningless repetitions as the gentiles do, for they suppose that they will be heard by their many words.

6 "So do not be like them; for your father knows what you need before you ask him.

Matthew 6: 1 - 8

10 For the sorrow that is according to the will of God produces repentance without regret, leading to salvation, but the sorrow of World produces death.

11 For behold what earnestness this very thing, this godly sorrow, has produced in you, what vindication of your selves what indignation, what fear, what longing, what zeal, what avenging of wrong! In everything you demonstrated yourselves to be innocent in the matter

12 So also I wrote to you, for it was not for the sake of the offender, nor for the sake of the offended, but that your earnestness of our behalf might be made known to you in the sight of God.
2 Corinthians 7: 10- 12

Meditation

According to some Christian tradition, Ash Wednesday is the first day of Lent, which comes the day after the last day of Marti Gras, the last day of the carnival season. Lent is the forty weekdays before Easter. During Lent, it is a custom to examine our lives, remembering who made us and where we will be at the end of our lives on earth. It is the time when we repent of our sinful ways and realize that God is eager to forgive. Our sins may be of omission of commission. Most of us, if not all of us have committed sins against others, such as lying, cheating, stealing, saying unkind words, or finding fault.

We have sinned against our own bodies by being gluttons or forming other bad habits that are harming the temple of our souls. Most of us, if not all of us, have committed sins of omission by failing to respond to the needs of others. On Ash Wednesday some people repent of their wrongful ways and give up certain foods and certain bad habits, at least during this season. We remember the love of our Heavenly Father and His willingness to forgive.

Thoughts for the Week

Lord, who through forty days for us didst fast and pray,
Teach us with to mourn our sins and close by thee to stay.
And thou with Satin did contend, and did the victory win,
O give us strength in thee to fight, in thee to conquer sin.

As thou didst hunger bear, and thirst, and teach us gracious Lord,
to die to self, and chiefly live by thy most holy word.
And through these days of penitence, and through thy passion tide,
yea in even more in life and death, Jesus, with us abide.

And abide with us, that so, the life of suffering over past,
and Easter of unending joy we may obtain at last.
Claudia R. Hermaman, 1873

Prayer

1 Be gracious to me, O God according to your loving kindness
according to the greatness of your compassion blot out my
transgressions.
2 Wash me thoroughly from my iniquity and cleanse me from my
sins!
3 For I know my transgressions and my sin is ever before me.
4 Against you, you only, have I sinned, and done that which is evil
in your sight so that you are justified in your presence and
blameless in your judgment.
5 Behold, I was born to iniquity and I have sinful since my mother
conceived me.
Psalm 51: 1 - 5

10 Create in me a clean heart Of God and renew a steadfast spirit
within me.
11 Do not cast me away from your presence and do not take your
holy spirit from me Amen
12 Restore to me the joy of your salvation and sustain me with a
willing spirit.
13 Then I will teach transgressions your way and sinners will be
converted to you.
Psalm51: 10 - 13

Palm Sunday

Scripture

28 After He had said these things, He was going on ahead, going up to Jerusalem.

29 When He approached Bethphage and Bethany, near the mount that is called Olive, He sent two of his disciples,

30 saying "Go in the village ahead of you; there, as you enter you will find a colt tied on which no one has ever sat; untie it and bring it here.

31 "If any one ask you, "Why are you taking it?" you shall say, The Lord has need of it."

32 So those who were sent went away and found it just as He had told them.

33 And as they were untying the colt its owner said to them, "Why are you untying the colt?"

34 They said, "The Lord has need of it."

35 They brought it to Jesus, and they threw their coats on the colt and sat Jesus on it.

36 As He was going they were spreading their coats on the road.

37 As soon as He was approaching, near the descent of the Mount of Olive the whole crowd of disciples began to praise God joyfully with a loud voice for all the miracles they had seen

38 Singing: "BLESSED BE THE KING WHO COMES IN THE NAME OF THE LORD; Peace and glory in the highest!"

39 Some of the Pharisees in the crowd said to Him, Teacher, rebuke your disciples."

40 But Jesus answered, "I tell you, "If these become silent the stones will cry out.".

Luke 19: 20 - 40

Meditation

On Palm Sunday, as Jesus rode into Jerusalem the crowd of disciples threw their coats, robes, and palm branches on the road in front of Jesus. Jesus was riding on the colt of a donkey. The crowd was singing, "Blessed is the king who comes in the name of the Lord." The palm branches were symbolic of victory and triumph. Jesus chose a donkey's colt as a statement of His mission on earth, as a servant and of peace. He did not choose a warhorse as a symbol of a political king to rule over Israel, nor as a military leader to defeat the Romans, as the Scribes and Pharisees expected the Messiah to be. Some of the Pharisees in the crowd told Jesus to rebuke the disciples, but Jesus told them that the stones would cry out and the disciples remained silent.

Jesus entered the temple and began to drive out those who were selling and said to them, "It is written," and "My house shall be a house of prayer, but you have made it a robber's den." The disciples and some of the people believed that Jesus was the Messiah and His kingdom was the kingdom of God at hand, and the kingdom of love, truth, and brotherhood, that would last forever. The priest scribes, and Pharisees thought that Jesus was a threat to their earthly physical kingdom. They tried to find a way to accuse Jesus of heresy and to find a way to destroy Him and His teachings.

Followers of the Christ, Jesus today invite the spirit of love and truth into their lives because of the life and teachings of Jesus, as we read, hear and remember the triumphant entry of Jesus into Jerusalem that Palm Sunday. Those who try to follow the teachings of Jesus do not rely on government or man-made doctrine to tell them what to believe or do. May the spirit of Christ dwell in us as we live our lives from day -o-day.

Thoughts for the Week

Hosanna, hosanna, the little children sang;
Through pillared courts and temples the lovely anthem rang.
To Jesus who had blessed them close fold to his breast,
the children sang their praises, simple and the best.

From Olivet mist, and exultant crowd,
the victor palm branches waving, and chanting clear and loud

the Lord of heaven and earth rode in a lowly state
Nor scold the little children should of his bidding wait.

"Hosanna in the highest," the ancient song we sing,
For Christ our redeemer, the Lord of heaven our king.
O may we ever praise him with heart and life and voice,
and in his full blissful presence eternally rejoice.
Jeanette Threlfall, 1874

Prayer

All praise to thee, for thou, O king divine, dist yield the glory that of right was thine
that in our darkened heart thy grace might shine:

Thou cam'st to us, in willingness of thought, by thee, the outcast and the poor were sought,
and by thy death was God's salvation wrought.

Let this mind be in us which was in thee, who was a servant that we might be free,
humbling thy-self to death on Calvary:

Wherefore by God's eternal purpose, thou are His exalted o'er all creatures now,
and given the name to which all knees shall bow:

Let every thought confess with one accord in heaven and earth that Jesus Christ is Lord,
and by God the Father by all adored:
Al-la-lu-ia! Al-la-lu-ia!   Amen
F. Bland Tucker, 1949

Easter

Scripture

50 Then a man named Joseph, who was a member of the council, a good and righteous man
51 (he had no concerns for their plan of action), a man from Arimathea, a city of the Jews, who was waiting for the Kingdom of God:
52 And he went to Pilot and asked for the body of Jesus.
53 And he took it down and wrapped it in linen cloth, and laid it in the tomb cut out of the rock no on had ever laid.
54 It was the preparation day and the Sabbath was about to begin.
55 Now the women who had come with him out of Galilee followed and saw the tomb and saw how His body was laid.
56 And they returned and prepared spices and perfumes. And on the Sabbath rested according to the commandment.
Luke 23: 50 - 56

1 But on the first day of the week, at early dawn they came to the tomb bringing the spices which they had prepared.
2 And they found the stone rolled away from the tomb,
3 but when they entered, they didn't find the body of The Lord Jesus.
4 When they were perplexed about this, behold, two men suddenly stood near them in dazzling clothing;
5 And the women were terrified and bowed their faces to the ground. The men said to them, "Why do you seek the living One among the dead?
6"He is not here but has risen. Remember how He spoke to you while He was in Galilee,
7 saying that the son of man must be delivered in the hands of sinful men, and be crucified and the third day rise again.
Luke 24: 1 - 7

Meditation

For generations the Israelites were looking for a Messiah to lead their nation to military dominance and security. When God came down in Jesus, the Christ, who taught of a different kingdom, a kingdom of love and peace, Jesus was a servant, a healer and a spiritual leader. Even his chosen disciples had difficulty understanding His mission on earth, even after walking with, talking and listening to Jesus for three years.

The Hebrew leaders realized that Jesus was not the type of leader that they wanted or expected. They plotted for ways to accuse him of blasphemy. They had him captured, tried Him and took Him before Pilate and demanded that He be crucified.

After the body of Jesus was wrapped in linen cloth and laid in the tomb of Joseph of Arimathea, His followers were confused and did not understand what Jesus had told them of life after death. On the first day of the week Mary Magdalene, Joanna, and Mary, the mother of Jesus, found the tomb empty. Angels were at the tomb and reassured them that Jesus was not dead but had risen as He told them when He was with them.

Jesus had to be killed, buried, and rise from the dead in order for man to comprehend that there is life after death. Although life after death has been prophesied and Jesus had told them that He would be crucified, rise on the third day and ascend to His Father in heaven, they did not believe until they said that He had risen and appeared before Him. God knew that through the death and resurrection of Jesus was the only way for man to truly believe. We now, through the scriptures can believe in existence with our Heavenly Father after death on earth. We worship and praise God with gladness and singing of the resurrection of Christians around the earth celebrate Easter as a time on newness of life. Christ.

Thoughts for the Week

Low in the grave he lay, Jesus my Savior,

Waiting the coming day, Jesus my Lord!

Vainly they watched his bed, Jesus my savior:
Vainly they sealed the dead, Jesus my Lord.

Death cannot keep its prey, Jesus my savior;
He tore the bars away, Jesus my Lord!

Up from the grave he arose, with a mighty triumph o'er his foes;
He arose, a victor from the dark domain,
And he lives forever with the saints to reign.
He arose! He A-rose! Hal-le-lu-iah! Christ arose!
Robert Lowery, 1874

Prayer

Almighty God,
Through Jesus Christ you overcame death
And opened to us the gates of everlasting life.
Grant that we, who celebrate the day of our Lord's resurrection,
May, by the renewing of your Spirit
Arise from the depth of sin to the light of righteousness;
Through Jesus Christ our Lord. Amen
The Lutheran Book of Worship, 1978

Pentecost

Scripture

1 When the day of Pentecost had come, they were all together in one place.
2 And suddenly there came from heaven a noise like violent rushing wind, and it filled the whole house where they were sitting.
3 And there appeared to them tongues of fire distributing themselves, and they rested on each one of them.
4 And they were all filled with the Holy Spirit and began to speak with other tongues, and the Spirit was giving them utterance.
Acts 2: 1 – 4

44 While Peter was still speaking these words, the Holy Spirit fell upon all of those who were listening to the message.
45 All the circumcised believers who came with Peter were amazed, because of the gift of the Holy Spirit had been poured out on the Gentiles also.
46 For they were hearing the speaking with tongues and exalting God. Then Peter answered,
47 "Surely no one can refuse the water for these to be baptized who have received the Holy Spirit just as we did, can he?"
Acts 10:44 -47

15"And as he began to speak, the Holy Spirit fell upon them just as He did on us at the beginning.
16 And remember the word of the Lord, how He used to say, "John baptized with water, but you will be baptized with the Holy Spirit."
Acts 11: 15, 16

Meditation

Pentecost was a Jewish festive day celebrating a harvest thanksgiving day, to be celebrated in the house of the Lord.
During the fifth week, the disciples began to preach the message of Jesus and the Kingdom of God to people of all nations in their own

language. Peter began to preach to the Gentiles. He said to them, "It is not for you to know times and epochs which the father has fixed by His own authority but will receive power when the Holy Spirit has come upon you; and you will be my witnesses both in Jerusalem, and in Judea and Samaria, and even unto the utmost part of the earth."
Acts 1: 7, 8

The apostles had gathered in one place for festival of the Pentecost when the Holy Spirit came upon them and they were made to speak in tongues with which the crowd of different nations could understand. The people were amazed and astonished. Jesus had commanded them to be his witnesses and through the Holy Spirit, the apostles were able to witness to all in their own language.

Peter preached to the men of Judea that God had said, through the prophet Joel, that he would send His spirit to all mankind. We today, receive the message that God sent through his Son, Christ Jesus. Christ's message is carried and preached all over the world by men and women filled with His spirit of truth and love. Through our spirit of truth and love we witness to those around us.

Thoughts for the Week

Come, Holy Ghost, our heart inspire, let us then influence pro; source of the old prophetic fire, fountain of life and love.

Come, Holly Ghost (for moved by thee the prophets wrote and spoke), unlock the truth, The self, the key unseal the sacred book,

Expand thy wings, celestial Dove, brood o'er our nature's night; on our disordered spirit move, and let there now be light.

God, through the Spirit we shall know if though within us shine, and sound, with all thy saints below, the depth of love divine.
Charles Wesley, 1740

Prayer

O Spirit of the living God, thou light and fire divine,
descend upon thy church once more, and make it truly thine.
Fill it with love and joy and power with righteous and peace,
till Christ shall dwell in human hearts, and sin and sorrow cease.

So shall we know the power of Christ who came this world to save;
so shall we rise with him to life which soars beyond the grave;
and earth shall with true holiness, which makes thy children whole;
till, perfected by thee, we reach creation's glorious goal.
Amen
Henry H. Tweedy, 1935

My Brother's Keeper

Scripture

6 The Lord said unto Cain, 'Why are you angry? And why has
your countenance fallen?'
7 "If you do well, will not your countenance be lifted up? And if
you do not do well, sin is crouching at the door; and
its desire if for you, but you must master it."
8 Cane told Abel his brother. And it came about when they were in
the field, that Cain rose up against Abel his
brother and killed him.
9 Then the Lord said to Cain, "Where is your brother? And he said,
"I do not know. Am I my brother's keeper?"
Genesis 4: 8, 1 9

2 It is the precious oil upon the head, coming down the beard, even
Aaron's beard, coming down upon the edge of the robes.
3It is like the dew of Hermon coming down the mountain of Zion,
for the `Lord commanded the blessing life
Forever.
Psalm 133: 1 – 3

13 Submit yourselves for the Lord's sake to every human
institution, whether to a king or one in authority,
14 or to governments as sent by him for the punishment of
evildoers and the praise of those who do right.
15 For such is the will of God that by doing right you may silence
the ignorance of foolish men.
16 Act as free men, and do not use your freedom as a covering for
evil, but use it as bond slaves of God.
17 Honor all people, love the brotherhood, fear God, and honor the
king.
1 Peter 2: 13 – 17

Meditation

In 1895, Charles Sheldon wrote a book entitled, 'His Brother's Keeper'. Stuart Duncan was the son of a wealthy iron ore mine owner in a small mining town in Kansas. Charles Sheldon was a minister of the Central Congregational Church in Topeka, Kansas. He read His Brother's Keeper, one chapter at a time at the evening church service.

When Stuart Duncan returned to the mining town, after a year in Europe, he learned that the miners had formed a labor union and were on strike in demand for better living conditions and for living wages. His lifelong friend, Eric Vassall, was the labor leader of the striking minors. A young lady, Rena Dwight, had left her wealthy family because of her Christian convictions to join the Salvation Army and help the miners and their families. The two of them did all that they could to help the miners and their families during the strike.

Stuart, Eric, Rena and the town's doctor, Doctor Saxon, worked together to get the miners and their families through a cold and bitter winter. After the death of Stuart's father, Stuart became owner of one of the mines and was quite wealthy. He struggled with his wealth and the poor conditions of the miners. Because of his own convictions and the lives of Eric and Rena, he was converted to the Christian way. His life was changed and he became a follower of Christ. He, through his life and his wealth, became empathetic with and joined the causes of the poor miners. All of them, including Doctor Saxon, risked all that they had, including their lives to bring a peaceful solution to the strike and improve the condition of the people.

In the end, the strike was ended and the miners returned to work. With the help of Stuart and his money, living conditions and the cause of humanity was greatly improved. Stuart, Eric, Rena, and Doctor Saxon were their brother's keeper.

Those who meditate on these thoughts are most likely caring, kind, and loving people. They are already their brother's keeper. We, as well as all Christians, can be our brother's keeper if we follow the teachings of Christ , our Lord and savior.

Thoughts for the Week

15 So when they had finished breakfast, Jesus said to Simon Peter, "Simon, son of John, do you love Me
more than these?" He said to Him, "You know that I love You."
He said to him, "Tend My lambs.
16 He said to him again a second time, "Simon, you of John, do you love Me?" He said to Him, Yes, Lord, You
know that I love You." He said to him, "Shepherd My sheep."
17He said to him the third time, "Simon, the son of John, "do you love Me." Peter was grieved because He said to him the third time, "Do you love Me?" And he said to Him, "Lord, "You, know all things; You know that I love you.
"Jesus said to him, "Tend My sheep.
John 21: 15 -17

Prayer

Lord, help me live from day to day in such a self-forgetful way,
That when I kneel to pray,
My prayer shall be for others.

Help me in all the work I do, to ever be sincere and true,
And know, that all I do for you
That needs be done for "others"

And when my work on earth is done, and when my work in heaven is begun
May I forget the crown I've won,
While thinking still of "others"

"Others" Lord, yes, "others"
Let this motto be,

Help me live for other, that I may live for Thee.
Amen

Scripture

6 Be anxious for nothing, but in everything by prayer and supplication with thanksgiving let your request be known to God.

7And the peace of God, which surpasses all comprehension, will guide your hearts and minds in Christ Jesus.

8Finally brethren whatever is true, whatever is honorable, whatever is right, whatever is pure, whatever is lovely, whatever is of good report, if there is any excellence and if there is anything worthy of praise, dwell on these things.

Philippians 4: 6 - 8

7 "Ask, and it will be given you, seek, and you will find; knock and it will be opened to you.

8For everyone who asks, receives and he who seeks, finds and to him who knocks it will be opened."

Matthew 7: 7, 8

5"When you pray, you are not to be like the hypocrites; for they love to stand and pray in the synagogues and on the street corners so that they may be seen of men. Truly, I say to you, they have their reward in full.

6 But you, when you pray go to your inner room, close the door and pray to your Father who is in secret and your Father who sees what is done in secret will reward you.   7

"And when you are praying, do not use meaningless repetitions as the gentiles do for they suppose that they will be heard for their many words.

8 So do not be like them, for your father knows what you need before you ask Him."

Matthew 6: 5 -8

Meditation

Prayer is communicating with God, not just speaking to him, but also listening to Him. We can have communion with God when we observe what he has given us in air, sunshine and rain, that allows us to see the cathedral that He has made of the plants, mountains, sea and with all of the actors; the birds, the fish, the animals and flowers that make up His beauty.

Jesus said that we will not be heard for our many words nor praying meaningless long prayers in public places to be heard of men. We commune with Him best when we are in a quiet place and listen to his still voice of nature, truth, healing and love. God knows our needs before we ask and has given them to us freely.

As Paul said in the letter to the people of Philippi, "Finally, brethren, whatever is true, whatever is honorable, whatever is right, whatever is pure, whatever is lovely, whatever is of good report, if there is any excellence and if there is anything worthy of praise, dwell of these things."

Thoughts for the Week

Dear Lord and Father of mankind, for give our foolish ways; re-clothe us in our rightful mind, in purer lives thy service find, in deeper reverence, praise.

In simple trust like those who heard, beside the Syrian Sea, the gracious calling of the Lord. Let us like them, without a word, rise up and follow thee. O Sabbath rest by Galilee, O calling of hills above, where Jesus knelt to share with the silence of eternity interpreted by love.

Drop thy still dews of quietness, till all our striving cease; take form our souls the strain and stress, and let our ordered lives confess. The beauty of thy peace break through the hearts our desire thy coolness of thy balm, let sense be dumb, let flesh retire; speak through the earth quake, wind, and fire. O still voice of

calm.
John Greenleaf Whittier, 1872

Prayer

9 Pray then this way: "Our Father, who's in heaven, hallowed be
Your Name,
10 "Your kingdom come, Your will be done, on earth as it is in
heaven.
11 "Give us this day our daily bread.
12 "And forgive us our debts, as we also forgive our debtors.
13 "And do not lead us into temptation, but deliver us from evil.
For Yours is the kingdom and the power and the glory forever.
Amen"
Matthew 6: 9 - 13

Mother's Day

Scripture

12 "Honor your father and your mother, that your days may be prolonged in the land which your God gave you.
Exodus 20:12

8Hear my son, your Father's instruction and do not forsake your mother's teaching
9 indeed, they are a graceful wreathe to your head and ointment about your neck.
Proverbs 1: 8, 9

26 When Jesus saw his mother, and the disciple whom He loved standing nearby, He said to his mother, "Woman, bole your son!"
27 Then He said to the disciple, "Behold, your mother!" From that hour the disciple took her into his household.
Matthew 19: 26, 27

Meditation

The ancient Greeks honored the mother of the Gods, with a special festival, "Mothering Sunday." This was celebrated by the early English Christians on the fourth Sunday in Lent, honoring England's mothers in the seventeenth century England.

Julia Ward Howe, poet, social reformer and Author of the "Battle Hymn of the Republic", suggested a day to honor mothers. She felt that the day to honor mothers should be dedicated to peace.

In 1907, Anna Jarvis began a campaign for a nationally recognized Mother's holiday, as we celebrate it now. Mother's Day was born when President Woodrow Wilson proclaimed the second Sunday in May as Mother's Day in 1914. Anna Jarvis also began the tradition of wearing a carnation to represent the sweetness, purity and endurance of motherly love. She chose the white carnation if her mother was deceased and the red carnation if her mother was still living.

Today, Mother's Day is celebrated around the world in honor of mothers. I am what I am today because of my mother's love, example and care. She loved everyone, including those who did not love her. President Wilson officially proclaimed Mother's Day a national holiday to be held on the second Sunday of May.

We love and honor our mothers because they first loved us. They gave us birth, nourished us, taught us and guided us as we developed into mature beings.

Thoughts for the Week

A blessing and prayer tribute to all mothers
Blessed be all mothers who have come into our lives.
Whose kindness, care and loving remains with us to guide
Your inspiration in us, made us strive in every way
Especially to remember helping others make their day.

Mothers, this little tribute
Flows directly from my heart
You are so loved and cherished
Invaluable. One and all, you are.
Susan Kramer

Prayer

I pray you'll be my eyes
And watch her where she goes
And help her t be wise
Help her let go

Every mother's prayer
Every mother knows
Lead her to a place
Guide her with your grace
To a place where she'll be safe

I pray she find your light
And hold it in her heart
As darkness falls each night
Remember her where you are

Every mother's prayer
Every child knows
Needs to find a place
Guide her with your grace
Give her faith so she'll be safe

Lead her to a place
Guide her with your grace
To a place where she'll be safe
Amen
Contributed by Christine

Faith

Scripture

20 And He said to them, "Because of the littleness of your faith;
for truly I say to you, if you have faith the size of a mustard seed,
you will say to the mountain. " Move from here to there", and it
will move; and nothing will be impossible to you.
Matthew 17:20

1 Therefore, having been justified by faith, we have peace with
God through our Lord Jesus Christ,
2 through whom also we have obtained our introduction by faith
into the grace in which we stand; and we exult in our hope of the
glory of God.
Romans 5:1, 2

1 Now faith is the assurance of things hoped for, the conviction of
things not seen,
2 for by it men of old gained approval. By faith we understand that
the worlds were prepared by the word of God, so that what is seen
was not made out of things that are visible.
Hebrews 11:1-3

Meditation

We all live by faith in God's laws. When we go to sleep at night
we believe that day will follow night, and that we will awaken in
the morning. We have faith that spring will follow winter, summer
will follow spring, and fall will not be far behind. By our faith, we
live a full and joyful life, as God wishes for us, if we adhere to
God's laws.

Jesus said that by our faith we could move mountains. Little did we
understand this until R. G. Latterno and others, through their faith
in God's Laws of physics, developed heavy earth moving
equipment and were able to move mountains from one place to

another. Through this faith, man has made highways through mountains and has built airport runways on top of them.
We have faith that if we follow God's instructions for taking proper care of our bodies that we will have a healthy, happy, life. By this faith we can leave the world healthy, happy, faithful children.

By our faith we know that God, through Jesus the Christ, wishes for us to live a full and joyful life. Through our faith in God's grace we know that when we come to the end of our lives we will enter eternal peace in God's love.

Thoughts for the Week

Faith while trees are still in blossom, plant the picking of the fruit: Faith can feel the thrill of harvest when the buds begin to sprout

Long before the dawn is breaking, faith anticipates the Sun. Faith is eager for the day light, for the work that must be done.

Long before the rains were coming Noah went and built and ark. Abraham the lonely migrant saw the light behind the dark.

Faith believes that God is faithful: God will be what God will be! Faith accepts the responding. "I am willing, Lord, send me.
Anders Frosterson, 1960

Prayer

Give me the faith that can remove and sink the mountain to the place; give me the childlike praying love,
which longs to build the house again, thy love,
let my heart o'er power, and all my simple soul devour.

Enlarge, inflame, and fill my heart with boundless charity divine, so shall all my strength exert and love thee with a zeal like thine, and lead them to thy open side, the sheep for whom the Shepherd died.
Charles Wesley, 1719

Memorial Day

Scripture

12 "This is my commandment, that you love one another, as I have loved you.
13 Greater loves has no one than this that one lay down his life for his friends."
John 15: 12, 13

11 "I am the good Shepherd; the good Shepherd lays down His life for the sheep.
12 He who in a hired hand, and not a shepherd who is not the owner of the sheep, sees the wolf coming, and leaves the sheep and flees, and the wolf snatches them and scatters them.
13 He flees because he is a hired hand and is not concerned about the sheep."
John 10: 11-13

16 "For God so loved the world, that He gave His only begotten Son, that whoever believes in Him shall not perish but have eternal life."
John 3: 16

Meditation

Jesus said, "Greater love has no one but to lay down his life for his friends." All over the world, men and women have given their lives defending the freedom and the lives of their friends and families. Our young men and women are placing themselves in harm's way defending freedom, their countrymen and all peace loving peoples.

Following the end of the Civil War, many communities set a day to mark the end of the war and as a memorial to those who gave their lives. The first Memorial Day was observed by liberated slaves at the historical racetrack in Charleston, South Carolina. Charleston was a former prison camp as well as a mass grave for union soldiers,who died while captive. A parade with thousands of freed blacks and union soldiers was followed by the singing of patriotic songs and a picnic.

In June of 1968, the united congress passed a Uniform Holidays Bill, which moved four holidays to a specified Monday, including Washington's Birthday, Memorial Day, Columbus Day and Veteran's Day. Christian church services of the Sunday prior to Memorial Day includes memories of men and women who have died defending our freedom and beliefs in respect for their devotion to America. The congress in 1950, requested the president to issue a proclamation calling for the of the United States to observe each Memorial Day as a day of prayer for permanent peace.

The commandments of God said to us, "You shall not murder." Yet we memorialize those who kill our enemies when they to kill us. God must desire for us to defend the innocent. As Christ said, "whoever causes one of the little ones who believe in Me to stumble, it would better for him to have a heavy millstone hung around his , and to drown in the depth of the sea."
Matthew 18: 6

Thoughts for the Week

The bugle echoes shrill and sweet
But not of war it sings to-day
The road rhythmic with the feet
Of men-at-arms who come to pray.

The roses bloom white and red
On tombs where weary soldiers lie
Flags wave above he honored dead
And martial music cleaves the sky

Above the wreath-strewn graves we kneel
They kept the faith and fought the fight

Through flying lead and crimson steel
They plunged for freedom and the right

May we their grandchildren, learn
Their strength, who lie beneath the sod,
We went through fire and death to earn
At least the accolade of God

In shining rank of rank arranged
The march the legion of the Lord
He is the Captain unafraid
The Prince of Peace… Who brought a sword
Joyce Kilmer

"Is life so dear, or peace so sweet, as to be purchased
at the price of chains and slavery? Forbid it, almighty
God! I know not what course others may take; but as
for me, give me liberty or give me death!"
Patrick Henry, 177

Prayer

Dear Heavenly father:
As we remember those who have made the ultimate sacrifice for
our freedom,
We think how they have followed in the footsteps of your Son, our
savior, Jesus Christ.
Please hold our service men and women in your strong arms.
Cover them with your sheltering grace and presence
As they stand in the gap of our freedom.
We also remember the families of our troops, and ask for
your unique blessings to fill their homes and
your peace, provisions and strength to fill their lives.
May the members of our armed forces be filled with courage to
face each day
and may they trust in the Lord's mighty power to accomplish each
task.
Let our military brothers and sisters feel your love and support.

In the name of Jesus.
Amen
Mary Fairchild (about com guide)

God's Promises to Man

Scripture

11 Now the earth was corrupt in the sight of God, and the earth was filled with violence.
12 God looked of the earth, and behold, it was corrupt; for all flesh had corrupted their ways upon the earth.
13 Then God said to Noah, "The end of all flesh has come before me: for the earth is filled with violence because of them; and behold, I am about to destroy them with the earth."
Genesis 6: 11-13

8 'Then God spoke to Noah and his sons with Him, saying,
9 "Now behold, I myself do establish My covenant with you, and with your descendants after you;
10 and with every living creature that is with you, the birds, the cattle, and every beast with you; of all that comes out of the ark, even every beast of the earth.
11 I establish My covenant with you; and all flesh shall never again be cut off by the water of the flood, neither shall there again be a flood to destroy the earth."
12 God said, "This is the sign of the covenant which I am making between me and you and every living creature that is with you, for all successive generations;
13 I set my bow in the cloud, and it shall be for a sign of a covenant between Me and the earth.:
Genesis 9: 9-13

Meditation

In the days of Noah, man had become evil. Their wickedness was in two ways, sexual lust and violence. Noah resisted evil and remained righteous and blameless before God and man. Because of his obedience to God, he was chosen to become responsible for man's new beginning on earth. After the flood, God promised

Noah that He would never destroy the world by flood. God set his rainbow in the sky as a reminder of this promise.

Today the world has become violent, filled with hate, sexual lust and self-destructive habits. Many people have desecrated their bodies, the temple of the soul, by unhealthy sexual practices, body destroying habits such as the use of drugs, excessive eating and use of alcohol and tobacco.

Noah believed in and remained obedient to Gods wishes. Noah was chosen by God to build an ark, save his family, some of each kind of animal and to start a new civilization. This obedience continued through Abraham, Isaac, Jacob, Joseph and Moses. We also have the promise that God will not destroy the world again by water. God came down in the body of Jesus and promised us that if we remained obedient to Him, through the example and teachings of Jesus, that at the end of our lives on earth, we would be with Him in the light of His love and eternal peace.

In the Psalms we find a promise of God;
4 He will cover you with His pinions, and under his wings you may seek refuge; His faithfulness is a shield and a bulwark.
5 you will not be afraid of the terror by night, or of the arrow that flies by day;
6 of the pestilence that stalks in darkness, of the destruction that lays way at noon.
7 A thousand may fall at your side and ten thousand at your right hand, but it shall not approach you.
Psalm 91" 4 -7

Many other promises of God are given to us in his Word. Another one is in Proverbs.
25 Do not be afraid of sudden fear nor of the onslaught of the wicked when it comes.   26
For the Lord will be your confidence and will keep your foot from being caught.
Proverbs 2: 25, 26

Thoughts for the Week

Standing of the promises of Christ my King
Through eternal ages let his praises ring:
Glory in the highest, I will shout and sing,
Standing on the promises of God.

Standing on the promises that cannot fail
When the howling storm of doubt and fear assail,
By the living word of God I shall prevail,
Standing on the promises of God.

Standing on the promises of Christ the Lord,
Bound to him eternally by love's strong cord,
Overcoming death with the Spirit's strong word,
Standing on the promises of God.

Standing on the promises I cannot fail,
Listening every moment to the Spirit' call,
Resting in my Savior as my all in all,
Standing on the promises of God.
R. Kelso Carter, 1885

Prayer

Almighty, everlasting, ever loving God, we praise You and are
eternally grateful for your promises to us that we may live a full
and peaceful life here on earth if we follow your teachings of those
who had faith and trust in You down through the ages. We are
grateful for the life and teachings of Your Son, Christ Jesus.
Because of Your promises to us we can rest and are reassured that
we will be with You in the warmth of Your love for eternity.
Amen

Man's Obedience to God

Scripture

3 Then Moses came and recounted to the people all the words of the Lord and all the ordinances; and all the people
answered with one voice and said, "All the words which the Lord has spoken we will do."
Exodus 24: 3

1 "So it shall be when all of these things have come upon you, the blessing and the curse which I have set before you, and you call them to mind in all nations where the Lord your God has banished you,
2 and you return to the Lord your God and obey Him with all your heart and soul according to all that I command
you today, you and your sons,
3 then the Lord your God will restore you from captivity and have compassion of you, and will gather you again from all the peoples where the Lord your God has scattered you.
Deuteronomy 30: 1- 3

10 "He opens their ears to instruction, and commands that they return from evil.
11 If they hear and serve Him, they will end their days in prosperity and their years in pleasure."
Job 36:10, 11

30 The God of our fathers raised up Jesus, who you had put to death by hanging on a cross.
31 "He is the one whom God exalted to His right hand as a prince and a Savior to grant repentance to Israel, and
forgiveness of sin.
32 And we are witnesses of these things and so is the Holy Spirit, whom God has given to those who obey Him."
Acts 5: 31, 32

Meditation

Noah remained obedient to God's will and was saved from perishing in the flood. He became the father of the new civilization. Abraham, Isaac, Jacob and Joseph obeyed and remained faithful to God. After the children of Israel were made captive of the Egyptians, Moses was born and his mother obeyed God by placing him in a basket on the Nile so that he was found by Pharaoh's daughter. Moses was saved from being killed with the other Hebrew boys and was raised up in the house of Pharaoh's family.

As Moses grew and became a man, he remained obedient to God and through his faith, led the children of Israel out of bondage and into the Promised Land. David remained obedient to God and led the Israelites back to obeying God and ruled the Hebrew nation.

Despite the loss of everything he had, including his health, Job remained steadfast and obedient to God. In spite of the urging of his friends to turn from God and his misery on earth, he remained obedient and faithful. Before his death he reclaimed his health and material things.

Job had prayed for his friends who had urged him to turn from God. Because of his faith and obedience, the Lord blessed his later years and Job died an old man and full of his days. Since God came to earth in Christ Jesus, many men and women have remained obedient to God and have lived a full and peaceful life. Some of them have helped create nations of peaceful, prosperous, free and peaceful life. Some of them have helped create notions of peaceful, prosperous, free and believing people. Since the days of Jesus, many have remained obedient to God through the teachings of Jesus, the Christ.

Thoughts for the Week

When we walk with the Lord in the light of his word,
What a glory he sheds on our way!

While we do His good will, He abides with us still,
And with all who will trust and obey.

Not a burden we bear, not a sorrow we share,
But our toil he doth richly repay:
Not a grief or a loss, nor a frown or a cross,
But is blessed if we trust and obey

But we never can prove the delight of his love
Until all on the alter we lay;
For the favor he shows, for the joy he bestows,
Are for them who trust and obey.

Then in fellowship sweet we will sit at his feet,
Or we'll walk by His side in the way;
What He says we will do, where He sends we will go!;
Never fear, only trust and obey.
John H. Sammis, 1997

Prayer

Take my life and let it be concentrated Lord to thee.
Take my moments and my days; let them flow in ceaseless praise.
Take my hands, and move at the impulse of thy love.
Take my feet and let them be swift and beautiful tor thee.

Take my voice and let it sing, always, only, for my King.
Take my lips and let them be filled with messages from thee.
Take my silver and my gold; not a might would I withhold,
Take my intellect, use every poser as thou salt chose.

Take my will and make it thine, it shall be no longer mine.
Take my heart, it is thine own:
it shall be thy royal throne, Take my love, my
Lord, I pour at thy feet thy treasure store.
Take myself and I will be ever, only, all for thee
Frank R. Havergal, 1872

Father's Day

Scripture

12"Honor your father and your mother that your days may be
prolonged in the land which the Lord Your God
gives you."
Exodus 20: 12

6 "For a child will be born to us, a Son will be given to us, and the
government will rest upon his shoulders;
and His name will be called Wonderful, Counselor, Mighty God,
Eternal Father, Prince of Peace."
Isaiah 9: 6

8"But now, O Lord, You are our Father, we are the clay, and You
are the Potter, and all of us are the works of Your hand."
Isaiah 64:8

Meditation

Since Abraham and Isaac, man has looked to his biological father
as well as his Heavenly Father for guidance, companionship,
protection and strength. In the year 1910, Sonora Smart Dodd
celebrated the first Father's Day in Spokane Washington. After the
death of her mother, she, along with her siblings, were raised by
their father. They celebrated the first Father's Day to honor and
remember their dad.

National Father's Day was begun by a joint Resolution of
Congress recognizing Father's Day in 1956 and 1966. Richard
Nixon established a permanent national observance of Father's
Day to be held on the third Sunday in June. I, to this day,
remember and rely on the teaching and guidance of my father in
making decisions and in the actions of my daily life. He will
continue to be with me and I will honor him until I am with my
Heavenly Father in the life after death.

A poem by an unknown author sums up a good description of how God made fathers.

God took the strength of a mountain,
The majesty of a tree,
The warmth of the summer sun,
The calm of a quiet sea,
The comforting arm of night,
The wisdom of the ages,
The power of the eagle's flight,
The joy of a morning in spring,
The faith of a mustard seed,
The patience of eternity,
The depth of a family need,
Then God combined these qualities,
And then there was nothing more to add,
He knew His masterpiece was complete,
And so, He called it - Dad.

Thoughts for the Week

Faith of our fathers, living still, in spite of dungeon, fire, and sword;
Our hearts beat high with joy when e'er we hear that glorious word!
Faith of our fathers, Holy faith!

We will be true to thee till death.
Faith of our fathers, we will strive to win all nations unto thee,
And through truth that comes from God,
we all shall then be truly free.
Faith of our fathers, Holy faith, we will be true to thee till death.
Faith of our fathers, we will love both friend and foe in all our strife,
And preach thee, to, as love knows how by kindly words and virtuous life.
Faith of our fathers, Holy faith, We will be true to thee till death.
Frederick W. Faber, 1849

Prayer

God of our fathers.
In your wisdom and love You made all things.
Bless these men,
that they may be strengthened as Christian fathers.
Let the example of their faith and love shine forth.
Grant that we, their sons and daughters,
may honor them always
with a spirit of profound respect.

Grant this through Christ our Lord
Amen
Author unknown

God's Requirement of Man

Scripture

6 With what shall I come to the Lord and bow myself before the God on high? Shall I come to Him with burnt offerings, with yearling calves?
7 Does the Lord take delight in thousands of rams, in ten thousand rivers of oil? Shall I present my first born for my rebellious acts, the fruit of my body for the sin of my soul?
8 He has told you, O man, what is good;
and what does the Lord require of you
but to do justice, to love kindness
and to walk humbly with your God?
Micah: 6 - 8

15 So when they had finished breakfast, Jesus said to Simon Peter, "Simon, son of John, do you love me more
than these?" He said to Him, "yes, Lord; You know that I love You." He said to him, tend my lambs."
16 He said to him a second time, "Simon, son of John, do you love me?" He said to Him, "Yes Lord, You
know that I love you." He said to him, "Shepherd my sheep."
17 He said to him the third time, "Simon, son of John, do you love Me?" Peter was grieved because He said to him
the third, "Do you love me?" And he said to Him, "Lord you know all things; You know that I love You." He said to him, "Tend my sheep.
John 21: 15 - 17

7 Beloved, let us love one another, for love is from God; and everyone who loves is born of God and knows God.
8 The one who does not love does not know God, for God is love.
9By this the love of God was manifest in us, that God has sent His only begotten Son into the world so that we might live through Him.
10 In this is love, not that we loved God, but that He loved us and sent His Son to be the propitiation for our sins.

11Beloved, if God has loved us we also ought to love one another.
I John 4: 7 - 11

Meditation

Since the beginning, man has believed that he had to make sacrifices and offerings of his animals and best earthly things in order to get God's attention and to please Him. Cain and Able offered Him offerings of their best yield of the fields or the best animal of the hunt. Abraham believed that God wanted him to sacrifice his son, Isaac, as a burnt offering, until God stopped him.

Most Primitive cultures offered their slaves and animals, as their own children to appease and please their gods. The Hebrews offered burnt offerings to please God. Micah revealed to us that God, who created man, animals, vegetation and everything beautiful in the world, did not want or need sacrifices and burnt offerings. Micah said that all God required of man was for man to do justly, love kindness and walk humbly with him.

A business executive was instructing his representatives that in order to be successful in their jobs and in their lives, there were three things that they should be. The first is to be kind. The second is to be kind. The third is to be kind.

Several years ago we had a maid who, if at all possible was the first to be there if someone was in trouble, sick, hurt or had a baby. She was the first deaconess to be present to comfort the grieving at the time of grief. That is why we called her Saint Georgia. We can please God by loving mercy, justice and being kind and to love one another as ourselves.

Thoughts for the Week

What does the Lord require for praise and offering?
What sacrifice, desire, or tribute bid you bring?
Do justly; love mercy; walk humbly with your God Rulers of earth, give ear, should you not justice know?

Will God your pleading hear, while crime and cruelty grow?
Do justly, love mercy; walk humbly with your God.

All who gain wealth by trade, for whom the workers toil, think not
to win God's aid, if greed your commerce soils.
Do justly, love mercy; walk humbly with your God.

How shall our life fulfill God's law so hard and high?
Let Christ endue our will with grace to fortify.
Then justly in mercy we'll humbly walk with your God.
Albert F. Bayly, 1968

Prayer

For Courage to Do Justice, O Lord,
Open my eyes that I may see the needs of others;
Open my ears that I may hear their cries;
Open my heart that they may not be without succor;
let me not be afraid to defend the weak because of the anger of the
strong,
Nor afraid to defend the poor because of the anger of the rich.
Show me where love and hope and faith are needed,
And use me to bring them to those places.
And so open my eyes and my ears
That I may this coming day be able to do some work for peace for
thee…
Amen.
Alan Paton, South Africa, 20th century

John the Baptist

Scripture

1 And an angel of the Lord appeared to him, standing to the right of the alter of incense.
2 Zacharias was troubled when he saw the angel, and fear gripped him.
3 But the angel said to him, "Do not be afraid, Zacharias, for your petition has been heard, and your wife Elizabeth
will bear you a son, and you will give him the name John.
Luke 1: 11 - 13

1 "Behold, I am going to send my messenger and he will clear the way before Me and the Lord, whom you seek, will suddenly come to His temple; and the messenger of the covenant, in whom you delight, behold, He is coming." says the Lord of host.
Malachi 3: 1

1 Now in those days John the Baptist came preaching in the wilderness of Judea, saying,
2 "Repent, for the Kingdom of heaven is at hand: For this is the one referred to by Isaiah the prophet when he said,
"THE VOICE OF ONE CRYING IN THE WILDERNESS , "
MAKE READY THE WAY OF THE LORD. MAKE HIS PATH STRAIGHT."
Matthew 3; 1 - 3

26 John answered them saying, "I baptize in water, but among you stands one whom you do not know.
27 It is He who comes after me, the thong of whose sandal I am not worthy to untie."
28 These things took place in Bethany beyond the Jordan, where John was baptizing.
29 The next day he saw Jesus coming to him and said, 'Behold the Lamb on God who takes away the sin of the world!"
John 1: 26 - 29

Meditation

John the Baptist (John the Baptizer) is regarded as a prophet by four religions: Christianity, Islam, Mandaeanism, and the Baha`i Faith. According to Luke, John the Baptist was the forerunner of Jesus Christ. John preached in the wilderness that the Kingdom of God was at hand and preached that his followers should repent of their sins and practice brotherhood. He preached that he baptized with water as an expression of repentance and to symbolically wash away their sins but that Jesus, the Christ, would baptize with spirit.

John found comfort in nature, eating grass, locusts and wild honey. He slept in holes in the ground, the dens of lions and bears. John was so deeply absorbed in praising God that the lions and bears recognized him as a prophet who cared for all creatures, so they would leave their caves to Him. John the Baptist sometimes fed the beasts, out of mercy, from his food. John the Baptist preached of love and called for people to repent and return to God. Because of his preaching, a conflict took place between him and King Herod because of the planned marriage of King Herod to his brother's wife. Because of his lust for Salome, he was persuaded to behead John the Baptist. The Saint-Jean-Baptiste Society in Canada made June 24th Saint John the Baptist Day. Saint John the Baptist Day has been celebrated by most French speaking cultures.

Thoughts for the Week

When Jesus came to be baptized by John,
He did not come for pardon but as the sinless one.
He came to share redemption with all who mourn their sins
to speak the vital sentence with which good news begins.

He came to share temptation, our utmost woe and loss,
for us and our salvation to die upon the cross
sor when the dove descended on Him, the Son of Man,
the hidden years had ended, the age of grace began.

Come, Holy Spirit, aid us to keep the vows we make;
this very day invade us, and every bondage break,
Come give our lives direction, the gift we covet most:
to share the resurrection that leads to Pentecost.
Fred Pratt Green, 1973

Prayer

Father in heaven
At the baptism of Jesus in the River Jordan
You proclaimed him your beloved Son
and anointed Him with the Holy Spirit.
Grant that all who are baptized in His name
may keep the covenant that they have made,
and boldly confess him as Lord and Savior,
Who with you and the Holy Spirit live and reign,
One God in glory everlasting.
Amen
The Book of Common Prayer

Freedom

Scripture

15 But to this day whenever Moses is read, a veil lies over their heart;
16 but when a person turns to the Lord, the veil is taken away.
17 Now the Lord is the Spirit, and where the Spirit of the Lord is, there is Liberty.
II Corinthians 3: 15 - 17

31 So Jesus was saying to those Jews who had believed Him, "If you continue in My word, then you are truly disciples of Mine;
32 and you will know the truth, and the truth will make you free."
33 They answered Him, "We are Abrahams descendants and have never been enslaved to anyone; how is it that
you say, "You will become free?"

34 Jesus answered them, "Truly, truly, I say unto you, everyone who commits sin is the slave to sin.
35 The slave does not remain in the house forever; the son does remain forever.
36 So if the Son makes you free, you will be free indeed."
John 8: 31 – 36

Meditation

On the fourth of July each year, we celebrate our political and economic freedom from England. During the fifteenth century, our ancestors sailed from England to the North American continent to obtain freedom or religion and worship. Prior to July 4, 1776, King George III of Great Britain continued to hold the American colonies in economic and political bondage. The thirteen colonies declared that they were independent states, formed a union and agreed on the Declaration of Independence, which was signed by all thirteen colonies.

On Independence Day, we in America think of freedom. On Passover and Easter, Jews and Christians, think of spiritual freedom. Jesus lived and died so that we might be free of spiritual bondage. Easter gives us freedom from high pressure and hard heartedness. Easter frees us of our self-centeredness, greed and self-righteousness. Easter allows us to live free in the love of God and to live for and to love others.

Easter frees us of hatred and blame. Christians are free to be forgiven, to be forgiving and compassionate to others. Easter gives us freedom from habits that consume and control us. Easter offers us freedom from separation from God. All of the personal hells of hate, hard heartedness, and self-centeredness find their antidote in Easter.

So, let us celebrate the freedom form human bondage that with God's help, our forefathers have given us. Also let us give thanks for the spiritual freedom Jesus has given us with his life, death and resurrection.

Thoughts for the Week

O beautiful, for spacious skies,
For amber waves of grain,
For purple mountain majesties
Above the fruited plane!
America! America! God shed His grace on the,
And crown thy good with brotherhood
From sea to shining sea!

O beautiful for pilgrim feet
When stern impassion'd stress
A thoroughfare for freedom beat
Across the wilderness.
America! America! God mend thy ev'ry flaw
Confirm thy soul in self-control
Thy liberty in law.

O beautiful for hero's proved
In liberating strife,
Who more than self their country loved,
And mercy more than life.
America! America! May thy gold refine
Till all success be nobleness,
And ev'ry gain divine.

O beautiful for patriots dream
That sees beyond the years
Thine alabaster cities gleam
Undimmed by human tears.
America! America! God shed His grace on thee.
And crown thy good with brotherhood
From sea to shining sea.

Katharine Lee Bates,1904

Prayer

May the glory of Independence Day
Remain in mind in heart
May we cherish our heard-won freedom
That it never fall apart.

Because those who walked before us
Believed in freedom's cause so much
We can carry forth a torch
Of honor and "In God we trust".

That first Independence Day
Now more than two centuries past
Must live forever in our thoughts
Never forgotten - never a lapse

It is a precious land we hold
In safekeeping for our children
That they, as we, may enjoy

Lives beautiful, worth living.

May God's blessing ever
Ring out over all our land
A toast of praises we raise today
Americans - join hands in heart!
Amen
Susan Helene Kramer

Growing Up

Scripture

41 Now His parents went to Jerusalem every year at the feast of the Passover,
42 and when He became twelve, they went up there according to the custom of the Feast;
43 and as they were returning, after spending the full number of days, the boy Jesus stayed behind in Jerusalem.
But His parents were unaware of it,
44 but supposed Him to be in the caravan, and went a day's journey; and they began looking for Him among their relatives and acquaintances.
45 When they did not find Him they turned to Jerusalem looking for Him.
46 Then after three days they found Him in the temple, sitting in the midst of the teachers, both listening to them and asking them questions.
47 And all who heard Him were amazed at His understanding and His answers.
48 When they saw Him they were astonished; and His mother said to Him, "Son, why have you treated us this Behold, your father and I have been anxiously looking for you"
49 And He said to them; "Why is it that you were looking for me? Did you not know that I had to be in my Father's House?"
50 But they did not understand the statement which He had made to them
51 and He went down with them and came to Nazareth, and He continued in subjection to them; and His mother treasured all these things in her heart.
52 And Jesus kept increasing in wisdom and statue, and in favor of God and man.
Luke 2: 41 - 52

17 You therefore, beloved, knowing this beforehand, be on your guard so that you are not carried away by the error of unprincipled men and fall from your own steadfastness

18 but grow in the grace and knowledge of our Lord and Savior
Jesus Christ. To Him be the glory, both now and to
the day of eternity. Amen
II Peter 3: 17, 18.

3 We ought always to give thanks to God, for your brethren, as it is
only fitting, because your faith is greatly enlarged, and the love of
each one of you toward on another grows even greater.
II Thessalonians 1: 3.

Meditation

Growing up spiritually is almost like growing up physically.
When we were newborn babies we were totally dependent on our
parents or other adult caregivers. We could not speak, we could not
feed ourselves, and we could not even turn over. Slowly, over
time, we grew in statue and mind. With the guidance and
assistance of our caregivers, we gained independence and were
able to care for ourselves.

When we were first born we were dependent both socially and
spiritually on others. We were self-centered, selfish, demanding
what we wanted and needed. As we received and gave love and
care we grew spiritually and socially. We continue to grow
spiritually. We need the spiritual nourishment from other
Christians and through Jesus Christ we all grow together to be true
Christians and more like Christ. Other infants and children who
were not born into Christian homes also grew up physically and
spiritually in their families and communities that believed in a
great spirit of truth and love, whether they be Hebrew, Indian,
African, Asian or any other ethnic group.

We continue to grow, as we teach and learn from other. We learn
from our children with their trust and unconditional love. We owe
it to our children to give them the physical and spiritual needs in
order for their complete growth into mature bodies and minds.

Thoughts for the Week

Father, we thank you. For you plant-d
Your holy name with in our hearts.
Knowledge and faith and life immortal
Jesus your Son to us imparts.

Lord, you and made all for your pleasure,
and give us food for all our days.
giving in Christ the brad internal;
yours is the power, be yours the praise.

As grain, once scattered on the hillsides,
was in the broken bread made one,
so from all lands your church gathered
into your kingdom by your Son.

F. Bland Tucker and others, 1939, 1982

Prayer

Our parent, by whose name all parenthood is known,
who in your love proclaim each family your own;
direct all parents, guarding well, with constant love
as sentinel, the home in which your people dwell.

O Jesus, who a child within and earthly home,
with heart still undefiled and to adulthood come;
our children bless in every place, that they may all
behold your face, and knowing you may grow in grace.

Blest spirit who can bind our hearts in unity,
and teach us so to find the love from self set free;
in all our hearts such love increase, that every home,
by this release, may be the dwelling place of peace.
F. Bland Tucker, 1939

Church

Scripture

13 Now when Jesus came into the district of Caesarea Philippi, He was asking His disciples, "Who do people say
that the Son of Man is?"
14 And they said, "Some say John the Baptist, and others, Elijah, but still others, Jeremiah, or one of the prophets."
15 He said to them, "But who do you say that I am?"
16 Simon Peter answered, "You are the Christ, the Son of the living God,"
17 and Jesus said to him, "Blessed are you, Simon Barjona, because flesh and blood did not reveal this to you, but My father who is in heaven.
18 I say to you that you are Peter, and upon this rock I will build My church, and the gates of Hades will not
overpower it."
Matthew 16: 13 - 18

42 They were continually devoting themselves to the apostles' teaching and to fellowship, to the breaking of
bread and to prayer.
Acts 2: 42

9God is faithful, though whom you were called into fellowship with His Son, Jesus Christ our Lord.
I Corinthians 1: 9

1 What was from the beginning, what we have heard, what we have seen with our eyes, what we have
looked at and touched with our hands, concerning the Word of Life–
2 and the life was manifested , and we have seen and Testify and proclaimed to you the eternal life, which was with
The Father and was manifested to us–
3 What we have seen and heard we proclaim to you also so the you

too may have fellowship with us; and indeed our
fellowship is with the Father, and with His Son, Jesus Christ.
4 These things we write, so that our Joy may be made complete.
I John 1: 1- 4

Meditation

Jesus asked the apostles who He was. After several guesses, Simon
Peter answered, "You are the Christ, the Son of the living God."
Jesus said to Peter. "I say to you that you are Peter, and upon this
rock I will build my church, and the gates of Hades will not prevail
against it." Peter recognized Jesus as the Christ, the Son of the
living God, and Jesus acknowledged Peter as a man. This man to
God relationship is what we have with God. All men and women
who have this relationship with God, regardless of religious
organization, creed, and ethnic origin of nationality are part of the
universal church of believers, (the Holy Catholic Church).

After the death of Jesus, believers formed fellowships and churches
in Israel, Asia and in Rome. These "Christians" were suppressed
and persecuted in Israel and in Rome. Despite the persecution, Paul
and the apostles spread Christ's teaching and the universal church
of believers grew. Following the decline of the Roman Empire the
churches underwent missionary activities and expansion. Man
organized churches in Asia and in Europe. The church in Rome
became the "Roman Catholic Church." From these churches many
other churches and denominations have developed because of
different beliefs, doctrines and cultures. There are people in every
church that worship their church organization, doctrine, custom and
social class. Some still worship and believe in Jesus' teachings of
love, charity and the brotherhood of all men. These remain in the
universal Church as Jesus taught and were ordained by Him but one
fellowship of those who believed in Him and follow His way of life.
We too may remain in the fellowship of the Father, Son and holy
Spirit of truth and love if we do not forget the teachings of Jesus
and do not let our pride, selfishness or greed interfere.

Thoughts for the Week

The church's one foundation is Jesus Christ our Lord;
we are his new creation by water and the word;
from heaven He came and sought us that we might ever be
his living servant people; by His own death set free.

Call forth from every nation, yet one o'er all the earth;
our charter of salvation: one Lord, one faith, one birth,
One holy name professing and at one table fed,
to one hope always pressing, by Christ's own Spirit led.

Though with a scornful wander the word sees us oppressed,
Schisms rent asunder, by heresies distressed,
yet saints their watch are keeping; their cries go up, "How long?"
but soon the night of weeping will be the morn of song.

Mid toil and tribulation, and tumult of our war,
we wait the consummation of peace for evermore;
till with the vision glorious our longing eyes are blest,
and the great church victorious shall be the church at res

We now on earth have union with God the Three in One,
and share through faith communion with those whose rest is won.
Oh, happy ours, and holy! Lord, give us grace that we
like them, the weak and lowly, on high may dwell with thee.
Samuel J Store, 1983

Prayer

Almighty and ever loving God, we worship You.
Thank You for coming to us that we might see and
understand the way to fellowship with You and with our
brothers and sisters in Christ.

May our lives shine so that others might believe in You and join
us.

We ask Your blessing on all those who believe in you and are in Your
Universal church.
Amen

Holy Spirit

Scripture

16"I will ask the Father, and He will give you another Helper, that
He may be with you forever;
17 that is the Spirit of truth whom the world cannot receive,
because it does not see Him or know Him, but you
Know Him, because He abides with you and will be in you"
18"I will not leave you orphans, I will come to you."
John 14: 16, 18

4 Gathering them together, He commanded them not to leave
Jerusalem, but to wait for what the Father had promised them,
"which", He said, "you heard from me;
5 for John baptized with water, but You will be baptized with the
Holy Spirit not many days from now."
6 So when they were coming together, they were asking Him
saying, "Lord, is it at this time You are restoring the
Kingdom of Israel?"
7 He said to them, "It is not for you to know times or epochs which
the Father has fixed by His own authority;
8 but you will receive power when the Holy Spirit has come upon
you; and you shall be my witnesses both in Jerusalem and in all
Judea and Samaria, and even in the remotest parts of the earth."
Acts 1: 4-8

22 But the fruit of the Spirit is love, Joy, peace, peace, patience,
kindness, goodness, forgiveness,
23 gentleness, self-control; against such things there is no law.
24 Now those who belong to Christ Jesus have crucified the flesh
with its passions and desires.
25 If we live by the Spirit, let us also walk by the spirit.
26 Let us not become boastful, challenging one another, envying
one another.
Galatians 5: 22-26
6 Do you not know that you are the temple of God and that the
spirit

of God dwells in you?"
I Corinthians 3: 16

Meditation

To know what the Holy Spirit is we must answer what God is.
Many people see God as human like man. Genesis 1: 2 reads;
"The earth was formless and void, and darkness was over the
surface of the deep, and the Spirit of God was moving over the
surface of the waters." God is spirit, truth and love.

John the Baptist was preparing the people for the coming of
Jesus; and he was preaching and saying, "After me one is coming
who is mightier than I and I am not fit to stoop down and untie
the thong of His sandals. I baptized you with water, but He will
baptize you with the Holy Spirit."
Mark 1: 7, 8

Jesus was born to Mary and His body was that of a man. The
Holy Spirit of God was in the mind of Jesus and Jesus' mind was
that of God.

At Pentecost the apostles received the gift of the Holy Spirit and
their minds were somewhat like that of Jesus (God), the spirit of
truth and love.

When we accept and believe in God through the example and
teachings of Jesus we allow the Holy Spirit, the Spirit of God, to
come into our mind and thoughts, and we grow spiritually more
like Jesus. The fruit of the Spirit if found in the letter of Paul's to
the Church of Galatia;
"But the fruit of the Spirit is love, joy, peace, patience, kindness,
goodness, faithfulness, gentleness, self- control, against such
things there is no law.
Now those who belong to Christ Jesus have crucified the flesh
with its passions and desires. If we live by the Spirit, let us walk

by the Spirit, let us not become boastful, challenging one another, envying one another.
Galatians 5: 22-23

Thoughts for the Week

Holy Spirit, Truth Divine
dawn up on this soul of mine;
word of God and inward light,
wake my spirit, clear my sight.

Holy Spirit, love divine, glow with
in this heart of mine; kindle every
high desire; perish self in thy pure fire

Holy Spirit, Power divine, fill every
nerve this will of mine; grant that I may
strongly live, bravely bear, and nobly strive

Holy Spirit, Right divine, King within my conscience reign; be my Lord , and
I shall be firmly bound, forever free.
Samuel Longfellow
1864

Prayer

Spirit of God, descend upon my heart;
wean it from earth; through all its pulses move;
stoop to my weakness, mighty as thou art,
and make me love thee as I ought to love.

I ask no dream no prophetic ecstasies,
no sudden rending of the veil of clay,
no angel visitant, no opening skies;
but take the dimness of my soul away

Hast thou not bid me love thee, God and King?
All, all thine own, soul, hart strength and mind.
I see thy cross; there teach my heart to cling.
O let me seek thee, and O let me find!

Teach me to feel that thou art always nigh;
teach me the struggles of the soul to bear,
to check the rising doubt, the rebelling,
teach me the patience of unanswered prayer.

Teach me to love thee as thine angels love,
one holy passion filling all my frame
The kindling of the heavenly descending dove.
Amen
George Cody 1867

New Commandment

Scripture

34 "A new commandment I give to you that you love one another, even as I have loved you, that you also love one another.
35 "By this all men will know that you are My disciples, if you have love for one another."
John 13: 34, 35

9 Let love be without hypocrisy. Abhor what is evil cling to what is good.
10 Be devoted to one another in brotherly love, give preference to one another in honor.;
11 not lagging behind in diligence, fervent in spirit, serving the Lord;
12 rejoicing in hope, persevering in tribulation, devoted to prayer,
13 contributing to the needs of the saints, preaching hospitality.
Romans 12: 9-13

Meditation

Most of us, if not all of us, have been through times when our spirits were down and our lives were going through a dark hour. We have lost a love one, lost our home, been in poor health, been in financial trouble or failed to achieve a goal. These are the times when we need a friend, a love one or even a stranger to see that we are in need, and show us love understanding and support as we resolve our problems. With their help, we may find a way to overcome our problems, reassure our lives with renewed feeling and strength and of being loved. When we give love and show compassion for others in their time of sorrow or need we lose the focus on our own problems as we concentrate on theirs. The satisfaction that we have helped others is joyful, rewarding and fulfilling in itself. As Jesus has commanded, "Love one another."

Thoughts for the Week

Jesus, Jesus, fill us with your love, show
show us how to serve the neighbors we have from you.

Kneels at the feet of his friends, silently washes their
feet, master who acts as a slave to them.

Neighbors are rich and poor, neighbors are black and
white, neighbors are near and far away.

These are the ones we should serve; these are the ones we should
love; all these are neighbors of us and you.

Love puts us on our knees, serving as though we are
slaves, this is the way we should live with you.
Tom Colvin, 1969

Prayer

Almighty and ever loving heavenly father,
you have commanded us to love one another as You have loved us.
May we remember what You have commanded as we walk from
day to day.
May we love and care for every one we meet.
Amen

Columbus Day

Scripture

7 "Ask and it will be given to you, seek and you will find; knock
and it will be opened to you.
8 for every one who asks re receives, and he who seeks finds, and
to him who knocks it will be opened.
Matthew 7: 7, 8

9 "So I say to you, ask and it will be given to you, seek and you
will find; knock and it will be opened to you.
10 For every one who asks, receives; and he who seeks, find, and
he who knocks, it will be opened.
Luke 11: 9, 10

15 And He said to them, "Go into the world and preach the gospel
to all creation.
16 "He who has believed and has been baptized shall be saved; but
he who has disbelieved shall be condemned."
Mark 16: 15, 16

1 If I speak with the tongues of men and of angels, but do not have
love, I have become a noisy gong or a clanging cymbal.
2 If I have the gift of prophecy, and know all mysteries and all
knowledge; and if I have all faith, as to remove
Mountains, but do not have love, I am nothing.
3 And if I give all my possessions to feed the poor, and if I
surrender my body to be burned, and do not have love, it profits
me nothing..."
1 Corinthians 13: 1 - 3

Meditation

Christopher Columbus was born in Genoa, Italy in about 1451.
Although he was Italian, he was associated with Spain, because he
was sponsored by the Catholic monarch and eventually in the

crown of Castile. With the fall of Constantinople to the Muslins in 1353 the land route to Asia was no longer an easy route.

Portuguese sailors began traveling south around Africa to get to Asia. By 1380, Columbus had developed a plan to travel to the West Indies, then construed as all South and East Asia. By sailing directly west to the "Ocean Sea." i.e. the Atlantic. Most of the Europeans believed that the world was flat. Most sailors and Columbus believed that the earth was a sphere.

In 1492, Columbus and his crew, in three small ships, sailed west and discovered some islands, which are now known as the Bahamas. After seven years, Columbus wrote to a friend at court, "In seven years, I, by the divine will make that conquest." While Columbus had always given the conversion of non- believers as one reason for exploration, he grew increasingly religious in his later years, he claimed to have visions, lobbied for a new crusade to capture Jerusalem, often wore Franciscan habits, and described his exploration to the Paradise "as part of God's plan which would soon result as the last judgment and the end of the world.

The order on the Knights of Columbus is the largest Catholic fraternal organization, named in order of Christopher Columbus and dedicated to the principles of charity, unity, fraternity and patriotism. Columbus Day is a holiday, celebrated in many countries in the Americas, commemorating the date of Christopher Columbus's arrival in the new world On October 12, 1492. Not all of the Americas celebrated as a day to be celebrated. Native Americans and some Latin Americans view the arrival of Columbus and those who followed led the way to mass genocide of Native Americans.

Thoughts for the Week

The things that haven't been done before,
Those are the things to try,

The Things That Haven't Been Done before

Columbus dreamed of an unknown shore
At the rim of the far-flung sky,
And his heart was bold and his faith was strong
And he ventured in dangers new,
And he paid no heed to the jeering throng
Or the fears of the doubting crew

The men will follow the beaten track,
With guidepost on the way,
They live and have lived for ages back
With a chart for every day.
Someone has told them it's safe to go
On the road he has traveled o'er,
And all that they strived to know before.

A few strike out without map or chart,
Where never a man has been,
From the beaten path they depart
To see what no man has seen.
There deeds they hunger also to do;
Though battered and bruised and sore,
They blaze the path for many, who
Do nothing not done before.

The things that have been done before
Are the tasks worthwhile to-day,
Are you one of the folks that follow, or
Are you one that shall lead the way?
Are you one of the timid souls that quit
At the jeers of a doubting crew,
Or dare you, whether you win or fail,
Strike out for a goal that's new?
Edgar A. Guest

Prayer

Creator God, this day is filled with many meanings and emotions.
For some it is a day of national pride.

For others it marks the coming of Europeans to land already settled.
For some it is a day of school or work.
Help us to discover the good that others have to teach us, their values and truths.
Help us to use our minds and hearts to become
aware of others and their needs so that this nation may unite in service of You.

Whenever the white man treats the Indian as they treat each other, then we will have no more wars.
We shall all be alike, brothers of one father, and one mother, with one sky above and one country around us, and one government for all.
Then the Great Spirit who rules above will smile upon the land and all people may be one people.
Amen
Columbus Day Prayer Service

David Livingston

Scripture

18 And Jesus came up to them, saying, "All authority has been given to Me in heaven and in earth.
19 "Go therefore and make disciples of all nations, baptizing them in the name of the Father and the Son and the Holy Spirit.
20 teaching them to observe all that I have commanded you; and lo, I am with you even to the end of the age."
Matthew 28: 18 -20

1 I will lift up my eyes to the mountains; from where shall my help come?
2 My help comes from the Lord, Who made heaven and earth.
3 He will not allow your foot to slip; He who keeps you will not slumber.
4 Behold, He who keeps Israel Will neither slumber nor sleep.
5 The Lord is your keeper; The Lord is your shade on your right hand.
6 the sun will not smite you by day, nor the moon by night.
7 The Lord will protect you from evil; He will keep your soul.
8 The Lord will guide your going out and your coming In. From this time forth and forever.
Psalm 121: 1 - 8

Meditation

David Livingston was born in Scotland in 1813. His father and mother were devout Christians. The family talked about things of Christ and His Kingdom. David, as a boy, worked, saved his money and completed his medical education in Glasgow. He was ready for some high call to which he give his utmost. The young Scotsman went to hear an address by a celebrated missionary, Robert Moffatt, and hear his vehement concern for perishing millions in Africa. The depth of David's soul rose up to meet the challenge of the missionary, especially which contained in the sentence, "I have sometime seen, in the morning sun, the smoke of a thousand villages where no missionary has ever been."

After hearing Doctor Moffatt, young David Livingston could not get his mind off a distant trail leading to Capetown and on to Kuruman, South Africa, and on to the great planes with its villages without the saving gospel. He studied the native language and was able to preach and teach in their native tongue. As he traveled among the villages, crowns of sick, suffering faces begged him to heal them. At night he would tell them the story of Jesus coming from heaven to earth to give his life on the cross so they might believe and be forgiven of their sins and inherit eternal life. David Livingston was eager to expose the horrors of the slave trade and to promote means by which to heal what he termed, "Cannot the love of Christ, carry the missionary where the slave trade carried the trade?" On his fifty ninth birthday, David made this entry in his journal, "My Jesus, my king, my life, my all, I again dedicate myself whole self to thee. Accept me and grant, O gracious Father, that ere this year is gone, I may find my task. In Jesus name I ask it. Amen, so be it. David Livingston.

Thoughts for the Week

How shall they hear the word of God, unless the truth is told?
How shall the sinful be set free, the sorrowful be consoled?
To all who speak the truth today, impart your spirit, Lord, we pray.

How shall they call to God for help unless they have believed?
How shall the poor be given hope, the prisoner be reprieved?
To those who help the blind to see, the light of light of love and charity.

How shall the gospel be proclaimed that sinners may repent?
How shall the world find peace at last if heralds are not sent?
So send us Lord, for we rejoice to speak of Christ with life and voice.
Michael Perry, 1092

Prayer

Go forth for God; go to the world in peace;
Be of good courage, armed with heavenly grace,
in God's good Spirit daily to increase,
till in the kingdom we see face to face.

Go forth for God; go to the world in love;
strengthen the faint, give courage to the weak;
help the afflicted ; richly from above
God's love supplies the grace and power we seek.

Go forth for God; go to the world in strength;
hold fast the good, be urgent in the right;
render to no one evil; Christ at length
shall overcome all darkness with his light.

Go forth for God, go to the world in joy,
to serve God's people every day and hour,
and serving Christ, our every gift employ,
rejoicing in the Holy Spirit's Power.
John R. Peacey, 1975

Mother Teresa

Scripture

34 "The King will say to the ones on the right, come you who are blessed of My Father, inherit the kingdom for you from the foundation of the world.
35 For I was hungry and you gave me something to eat; I was hungry and you gave me something to drink; I was a stranger and you invited me in;
36 naked and you clothed me; I was sick and you visited me, I was in prison and you came unto Me.
37 "Then the righteous will answer Him, "Lord when did we see you hungry and feed You, thirsty and gave You something to drink?"
38 When did we see you a stranger and invite You in, or naked and cloth You?
39 When did we see You sick, or in prison and come to You?
40 "The King will answer and say to them, "Truly I say to you, to the extent that you did it to the least of these brothers of Mine, even the least of them, you did it to Me."
Matthew 25: 34 - 40

37 "He who loves his father and mother more than Me is not worthy of Me, and he who loves his sons and daughters more than Me is not worthy of Me.
38 And he who does not take up his cross and follow after Me is not worthy of Me.
39 "He who has found his life will lose it, and he who has lost his life foe My sake will find it,"
Matthew 10: 37 -39

Meditation

Mother Theresa was born in 1910 in Scopie, Yugoslavia. Her father died when she was eight years old. After her father's death, her mother raised her as a Roman Catholic. She became fascinated with the lives of missionaries and their service. By the age of twelve she felt that she should commit herself to a religious life. She left home at the age of eighteen to join the Sisters of Lorto as a missionary. She took her religious vows as a nun in 1931. At that time she chose the name, Theresa, after Theresa de Lisieux, the patron saint of missionaries.

One day, Mother Theresa found a dying woman in front of the Calcutta Hospital. She stayed with the woman until she died. She then devoted her life to help the poorest of the poor of India, thus getting the name, "the saint of the Gutter." She founded an order of nuns called The Missionaries of Charity in Calcutta, India.

In 1952, she founded the Nina Holiday Home in the former temple in Calcutta. There they would care for the dying Indians that were found on the street. Mother Theresa saw Jesus in every one she met. She wanted them to die in peace and dignity.

Mother Theresa's confessor said, "The meaning of her whole life was a person, Jesus. " The general postulator of her cause of benefaction concluded, "I have to say , in synthesis, why she is raised to the honor of the alter, I reply: Because of her personal love for Jesus, which she lived in such an intense way as to consider her-self to be His bride. Hers was a Jesus centered life."

To the question, who is Jesus to me? The founder of the missionaries of Charity replied with a series of titles, "Jesus is a life that must be lived"; "He is a love that must be loved;" "He is the joy; that joy that must be shared", "He is the sacrifice that must be offered", "and He is the peace that must be taken." The preacher recalled one of Mother Theresa's best known phrases, "The fruit of Love is service, and the fruit of service is Peace."

Thoughts for the Week

Do it anyway
People are unreasonable,
illogical and self-centered;

Forgive them anyway.

If you are kind
People may accuse you of selfish ulterior motives;
Be kind anyway.

If you are successful,
You will win some false friends and some enemies;
Succeed anyway.

If you are honest and frank,
People may cheat you;
Be honest anyway.

When you spend years building,
Someone could destroy over night;
Build anyway.

The good you do today,
People will often forget tomorrow;
Do good anyway.

Give the world the best you have,
And it may never be enough;
Give the world the best you've got anyway.
Mother Theresa

Prayer

Dear Jesus,
Help us to spread your fragrance everywhere we go.
Flood our souls with your spirit and life.
Penetrate and possess our whole being so utterly,
that our lives may only be a radiance of yours.
Shine through us,
and be so in us,
that every soul we come in contract with
may feel your presence in our soul.

Let them look up and see no longer us,
but only Jesus!
Stay with us,
and then we shall begin to shine as you shine;
so to shine as to be a light to others;
the light O Jesus, will be all from you,
none of it will be ours;
it will be you, shining on others through us.
Let us thus praise you in the way you love best,
by shining on those around us.
Let us preach you without preaching,
not by words but by example,
by the catching force,
the sympathetic influence of what we do,
the evident fullness of the love our hearts bear to you.
Amen.
Mother Teresa

Albert Schweitzer

Scripture

18 Now as Jesus was walking by the Sea of Galilee, He saw two brothers Simon who was called Peter and Andrew his brother, casting a net into the sea; for they were fisherman.
19 And He said to them, "Follow me, and I will make you fishers of men."
20 Immediately they left their nets and followed Him.
Matthew 4: 18 0 20

5 Thomas said to him, "Lord, we do not know where You are going, how do we know the way?"
6 Jesus said to him, "I am the way, and the truth, and the life; no one comes to the Father but through Me.
7 If you had known Me, you would have known My Father also; from now on you know Him, and have seen Him."
John 14: 5 - 7

16 "I will ask My Father and He will give you another Helper, that He may be with you forever;
17 that is the Spirit of truth, who the world cannot receive, because it does not see Him or know Him, but you know Him because He abides with you and will be in you.
John 14: 16, 17

Meditation

Albert Schweitzer was born in Germany in 1875. His father was the local pastor in the Lutheran Church. He spent most of his childhood in Gunsbach, Alsace, where his father taught him music. He later studied philosophy and music in Paris. In 1899, he published The Religious philosophy Of Kant, which earned him his PhD in Theology. He became pastor at the Church Saint - Nicholas of Strasbourg. In 1905, at the age of thirty, he answered the call "The Society of Evangelical Missions of Paris", who was looking for a medical doctor. He began his medical studies and later left Alsace for Gabon, Africa, which was French at that time.

As a young theologian he published The Quest of the Historical Jesus, which gained his reputation as a theologian. Schweitzer established his reputation as a New Testament scholar with other theological studies including his medical dissertation The Psychiatric Studies of Jesus, and The Mysticism of Paul the apostle. Schweitzer said, "The only ones among you who are really happy are those who have sought and found how to serve."

Schweitzer's world vies was based on his idea of reverence for life, which he believed to be his greatest contribution to mankind. His view was that the western civilization was in decay because of gradually abandoning its ethical foundations. It was his firm conviction that the respect for life is the greatest principle. He said, "True philosophy must start from the immediate and comprehensive fact of consciousness...I am life that wants to live in the midst of life that wants to live." Respect for life, resulting from contemplation on one's own conscious will to live, leads one to live in the service of other people and every living creation.

Schweitzer was much respected for putting his theory into practice in his own life. Schweitzer considered his work as a medical missionary in Africa to be his response to Jesus call to become "fishers of men" but also a small response historic guilt of the Europeans. "Who can describe the injustice and cruelties that in the course of centuries they, the colored people, have suffered at the hands of the Europeans? If record could be completed of all that has happened between the white and the colored races, it would make a book containing numbers of pages which the readers have to turn over unread because the contents would be too horrible."

Schweitzer states, "I will not enumerate all the crimes that have been committed under the pretext of justice, people robbed native inhabitants of their land, made slaves of them, let loose the scum of mankind upon them. Think of the atrocities that were perpetrated upon people made subservient to us, how systematically we ruined them with our alcoholic "gifts," and everything else we have done. We decimated them, and then, by the stroke of a pen, we take their land so they have nothing left at all...If all this opposition and all this sin and shame are perpetrated under the German God, or the American God, or the British God and if our states do not feel obligated first to lay aside their claim to be "Christian"--- then the name of Jesus is blasphemed and made a mockery. And the Christianity of our states are blasphemed and made a mockery before the poor people. The name of Jesus has become a curse, and our Christianity – yours and mine has become a falsehood and a disgrace, if the crimes are not atoned for in the very place where were instigated. For every person who committed an atrocity in Jesus' name some one must step in to help in Jesus' name; for every person who is robbed, someone must bring a replacement; for everyone who is cursed, someone must bless…And now, when you speak about missions, let this be your message; We must make atonement for all the terrible crimes we read of in the newspapers. We must make atonement for the still worse ones, which we do not read about in the papers, crimes that are shrouded in the silence of the jungle night."

He thought Gabonese independence came too early, without adequate education or accommodations to local circumstances. Ed Berman quotes Schweitzer speaking these lines, "No society can go from a primeval directly to and industrial state with losing the leavening that time and an agricultural period allow.

On Good Friday, 1913, Albert Schweitzer and his wife set sail from Bordeaux for Africa where Schweitzer established on the grounds of the Labarene Station of the Paris Missionary Society, his medical practice. From the first, where Schweitzer's hospital was a broken down hen coop, natives flocked by foot, by improvised stretchers, by dugout canoe to Lambarene for medical attention. Some of his most ardent admirers insisted that he was a jungle saint, even a modern Christ, but Schweitzer rejected such adulteration; he held that his own spiritual life was its own reward and that works redeemed him. He took the search for the good life seriously. For him it held profound religious implication. "Anyone can rescue his human life; he once said, "Who seizes every opportunity of being a man by personal action, however unpretending, for the god of fellow men who need the help of fellow man."

Thoughts for the Week

Lord, whose love through humble service bore the weight of human need, who upon the cross, forsaken offered mercy's perfect deed: we, your servant , bring the worship not of voice alone, but heart, consecrating to your purpose every gift that you impart.

Still your children wander homeless; still the hungry cry for bread; still the captive long for freedom; Still in grief we mourn our dead. As, O Lord, your deep compassion healed the sick and freed the soul, use the love your Spirit kindles still to save and make us whole

And we worship, grant us vision, till your love revealing light in its height and depth and greatness dawn upon quickened sight, making known the needs and tireless serving your abundant life to save.

Called by worship to your service, forth in your dear name
we go to the child, the youth, the aged,
Love in living deeds to show; hope and health, good will and
comfort, aid, and peace we give that your servants,
Lord. In freedom may your mercy know, and live
Fred Pratt Green, 19 71

Prayer

Dear Lord and Father of mankind, forgive our feverish ways;
Re-clothe us in our rightful mind,
In purer lives thy service finds, in deeper reverence praise.

In simple truth like theirs who heard,
Beside the Syrian Sea the gracious calling
Of the Lord, let us, like them without a word, rise up and follow
thee.
Amen
John Greenleaf Whittier, 1872

R. G. Letourneau

Scripture

18 And Jesus rebuked him, and the demon came out of him, and the boy was cured at once.
19 The disciples came to Jesus privately and said, "Why could we not drive it out?"
20 And He said to them. "Because of the littleness of your faith; for I truly I say to you, if you have faith the size a mustard seed, you will say to the mountain, "Move from here to there," and it will move, and nothing will be impossible to you."
Matthew 17: 18 - 20

31 Do not worry then, saying, "What shall we eat?" Or "What shall we drink?" Or "What will we wear for clothing"
32 "For the gentiles seek all these things; for you heavenly Father knows that you need all these things
33 "But seek first His kingdom and His righteousness, and all these things will be added to you.
34 "So do not worry about tomorrow, for tomorrow will care for its self. Each day has enough troubles of its own."
Matthew 6: 31 - 34 s

11 When I was a child, I used to speak as a child, think like a child, reason like a child. When I became a man, I did away with childish things.
12 For now we see through a mirror dimly, but then face to face; now I know in part, but then I will know fully just as I also have been fully known.
13 But now faith, hope, love, abide these three; but the greatest of these is love.
I Corinthians 13: 11 - 13

Meditation

Robert G. Letourneau was born on November 30, 1888 to godly parents. From infancy he heard the gospel. Early in his life, he rejected gospel but through the prayers of his parents he was won to Christ at the age of sixteen. At the age of thirty he dedicated his life to be God's businessman. His commitment was dimmed by his love for machines, but by the grace of God that commitment continued for fifty years.

Many books have been published about R. G. Letourneau's life, including his best-selling autobiography 'Mover of Men and Mountains'. We cannot tell how many have come to faith in Christ through his ministry in Liberia, West Africa, Peru, South America, and North America.

Letourneau University, which he and his wife founded, may well prove to be one of his greatest accomplishments, as his influence is multiplied and spread throughout the world by dedicated Christian young people who have studied at the college. His outreach for God's aid to individuals and organizations by the Letourneau Foundation has reached people worldwide, His life's verse was Matthew 6: 33; seek you first the kingdom of God and His righteousness and all these things will be added unto you.

R. G Letourneau had faith in his own imagination, ability and faith in God's truths would show him the way. He designed and built beyond the imagination of ordinary men. He introduced into the earth moving industry the largest earth moving machines and materials the industry had ever known. He also developed the largest rubber tire which today is universally accepted. He also invented and developed the large electric driven wheel, which is used on the large machines of his huge offshore drilling platforms. These are used to support the machines that drill for the rich petroleum reserves under the seas around the World. He demonstrated his concern the gospel witnessed by establishing regular chapel services and by employing full time chaplains in his manufacturing plants.

R. G Letourneau continued his role as a Christian layman. He developed projects in Liberia with the goal of goal of colonization, land development, agriculture, livestock, and evangelism. He held many respected positions throughout his life as a Christian layman leader on the Christian and Missionary Alliance Church, president of the Christian Business Men's Association and president of the International Gideon Society.

As a multimillionaire, Letourneau said that his money came in faster than he could give it away. Letourneau was convinced that he could not out-give God. "I shovel it out", he would say, "and God shovels it back, but God has the biggest shovel."

Letourneau's example reminds us that we too can be mountain movers. As the Great Physician said in Matthew 17: 20, "To tell the truth, if you have faith as small as a mustard seed, you can say to this mountain, "move from here to there and, and it will move." "Nothing will be impossible for you", R. G. Letourneau once said: "You will never know what you can accomplish until you say a great big yes to the Lord."

Thoughts for the Week

Give me the faith that can remove and sink the mountain to a plane,
give me the childlike praying love which longs to build the house again;
thy love let it my heart o'er power, and all my simple soul devour.

I would the precious time redeem and longer live for this alone,
 to spend and to be spent for them who have not my savior known;
fully on these mission power , and only breath, to breath thy love.

My talents, gifts, and graces, Lord, into thy blessed hand receive;
let me live to preach thy word, and let me to thy glory live;
my every sacred moment spend in publishing the sinner's Friend.

In large, inflame, and fill my heart with boundless charity divine,
so shall my all my strength exert and love them with a zeal like
thine,
and lead them to thy open side,
the sheep for whom the shepherd died.

Prayer

Inspire the living faith which who o'er receive,
the witness in themselves thy love and consciously believe
the faith that conquers all, and doth the
mountains move, and saves on Jesus call, and
perfects those in love.
Amen
Afro-American Spiritual

Mahatma Gandhi

Scripture

19 Now listen to me; I will give you council; and God be with you. You are the people's representative before God, and you bring the disputes to God,
20 them teach them the statues and the laws, and make known to them the way in which they are to walk and the work they are to do.
21 "Furthermore , you shall select out of all the people able men who fear God, men of truth, those who hate dishonest gain; and you shall place these over them as leaders of thousands, of hundreds, of fifties, of tens.
Exodus 18: 10 -21

1 "Do not let your heart be troubled: believe in God, believe also in Me.
2 "In my heart there many dwelling places; if it were not so, I would have told you; for I go to prepare a place for you.
3 "If I go to prepare a place for you, I will come again and receive you to Myself, that where I am, then you may be also.
4 "And you know the way where I am going."
5 Thomas said to them, "Lord, we do not know where You are going, how do we know the way?"
6 Jesus said to him, "I am the way, and the truth, and the life; no one comes to the Father but by Me".
John 14: 1 - 6

Meditation

Mahatma Gandhi was a political and spiritual leader of India and the Indian independence movement. He was the pioneer of the philosophy that is largely concerned with truth and resistance to evil through active non-violent resistance, which led India to independence and inspired movements of civil rights and freedom across the world. Gandhi is commonly known in India and across the world as the Mahatma; "the great soul". Mahatma Gandhi was born in 1869 in a Hindu family. Mahatma Gandhi's mother was a devout Hindu. Gandhi learned from an early age tenets of non-injury to living things, vegetation, fasting for self-purification and natural tolerance between members of various creeds and sects.

At the age of eighteen, Gandhi went to University College in London, studied law and trained as a barrister. His time in London was influenced by a vow he made to his mother, to observe the Hindu precepts of abstinence from meats, alcohol and promiscuity. He was influenced by the Theological Society, which had been founded to further universal brotherhood. He began to read works of and about Hinduism, Christianity, Buddhism, Islam and other religions. In South Africa, Gandhi found discrimination directed at Indians. He was thrown off a train refusing to move from the first class coach while holding a first class ticket. He was beaten by a stagecoach driver for refusing to travel on the footboard to make room for European passengers. He was barred from many hotels. He awakened to the social injustice and helped his subsequent social activism.

When Gandhi returned to India, a white mob attacked him and tried to lynch him. He refused to press charges against any member of the mob, stating that it was one of his principles not to seek regress for a personal wrong. Non-corporation and peaceful resistance was Gandhi's "weapon" in the fight against injustice. The massacre of civilians by British troops caused deep trauma to the nation, leading to increased public anger and acts of violence. Gandhi criticized both the action of the British and the retaliation violence of the Indians. Due to Gandhi's influence and platform of peaceful resistance and non-violence, India was finally given independence by Briton. His fasting to death finally awakened the conscious of Briton to end British domination of India. On January 3, 1948, Mahatma Gandhi was shot and killed while having his nightly public walk by an assassin.

Gandhi's memorial in New Deli bears the epigraph, "He Ran", which may be translated, "Oh God". These were Gandhi's last works. Gandhi dedicated his life to the purpose of discovering truth. He tried to achieve this by learning this by his own mistakes. He called his autobiography, The Story of My Experiences with Truth. Gandhi stated that the most important battle to fight was overcoming his own demons, fear and insecurities. Gandhi summarized his beliefs when he first said "God is truth." To Gandhi, "Truth is God."

Gandhi was quoted as saying. "When I despair, I remember that all through history the way of truth and love has always won...An eye for and eye makes the whole world blind...As soon as we lose moral basis, we cease to be religious...There is no such thing as religion overriding morality...Man, for instance cannot be untruthful, cruel, and incontinent and claim to have God on his side." When he was asked whether he was a Hindu he replied, "Yes, I am, I also am a Christian, a Muslim, a Buddhist and a Jew...God fearing death has no terror."

Mahatma Gandhi said to his friend and missionary to India, E. Stanley Jones, "O, I don't reject your Christ, I love your Christ. It is that so many of your Christians are unlike your Christ... An ounce of practice is worth a ton of preaching...But for my faith in God, I should have been a raving Maniac: God as truth had been for a treasure beyond price. May He be to every one of us."

Thoughts for the Week

God of love and God of power, grant us in the burning hour
Grace to ask these gifts of thee, daring hearts and spirits free.
God of love and God of power, thou hast called us for this hour.
We are not the first to be banished by our fears from thee;

Give us courage; let us hear heavens trumpets ringing clear.
God of love and God of power, thou hast called us for this hour.
All our lives belong to thee, thou our final loyalty;

Slaves are we when e'er we share that devotion anywhere.
God of love and God of power, thou hast called us for this hour.
God of love and God of power, make us worthy of this hour;
Offering lives if it's thy will, keeping our spirits still.
God of love and God of Power, thou hast called us for this hour.

Gerald H. Kennedy, 1939

Prayer

For the healing of the nation, Lord, pray with one accord;
for the just and equal sharing of the things that earth affords
to the life in action help us rise and pledge our word,
help us rise and pledge our word.

Lead us forward into freedom; from despair your world release,
that, redeemed from war and hatred, all may come and go in peace,
show us through care and goodness fear will die and hope increase,
fear will die and hope increase.

All that kills abundant living, let it from the earth be banned;
pride of status, race or schooling, dogmas that obscure your plan.
In our common quest for justice may we hallow life's brief span,
may hallow life's brief span.

You, Creator God, have written your great name on human-kind;
for our growing in your likeness bring the life of Christ to mind,
by our response and service earth its destiny may find,
earth its destiny may find.

Fred Kaan, 1965

Robert Lawrence

Scripture

1 The Lord is my shepherd, I shall not want.
2 He makes me lie down in green pastures; He leads me beside the quiet waters.
3 He restores my soul; He guides me in the paths of righteousness For His name's sake.
4 Even though I walk through the valley of the shadow of death, I fear no evil, for You are with me...
5 You prepare a table before me in the presence of my enemies You have anointed my head with oil; My cup overflows.
6 Surly goodness and loving kindness will follow me all the days on my life, and I will dwell in the house of the Lord forever
Psalm 23: 1 - 6

19 "Go therefore and make disciples of all nations, baptizing them in the name of the Father and the Son and
Holy Spirit,
20 teach them to observe all that you commanded; and lo, I will be with you always, even to the end of the age."
Matthew 28: 19 - 20

14 You are the light of the world. A city set on a hill cannot be hidden;
15 nor does anyone light a lamp and put it under a basket; but on the lamp stand, and it gives light to all who are in the house.
16 "Let your light shine before men in such a way that they may see your good works, and glorify your Father who is in Heaven."
Matthew 14 -16

Meditation

Robert Lawrence was born in northern Alabama in 1898. His father and mother were devout Christians and raised Robert and eight other children on a farm. They were taught to respect all of

God's creation. Robert and his brothers and sisters went to a Methodist church service on Sunday morning and a Baptist Sunday school on Sunday afternoon.

Robert was called to preach Christian beliefs and after high school, entered Birmingham Southern College to become a Methodist preacher. He met a Methodist preacher's daughter and when he finished college they were married. They entered the Christian ministry in southern Alabama.

Brother Lawrence's Christian spirit showed wherever he was, in town, in a fishing boat, in people's homes, in the pulpit, or wherever he might happen to be. His love for people shined to all; regardless religion, color, creed, social status, or denomination. One of his Methodist churches was supported by a Jewish businessman. He carried the message of Christ's love and truth wherever he went.

Brother Lawrence witnessed to the poor, handicapped, merchants, judges governors, and to those in prison. Mr. Anderson was in jail for murder. He had killed a man when they were drinking and gambling. They got into a fight and Mr. Anderson got the first shot that killed the other man. Mr. Anderson was sentenced to die in the electric chair.

One day, Brother Lawrence was visiting the jail and witnessed to Mr. Anderson. After Brother Lawrence read the bible and prayed, Mr. Anderson truly repented of his sins and asked for forgiveness. God would forgive him and he could let Jesus come into his life. Jesus would help him resist temptation, live a better life and inherit eternal life. Mr. Anderson dropped to his knees, cried and let Jesus take charge of his life. He felt peace that he had never felt before.

Later Brother Lawrence talked with the judge and with the jailer. One day, they brought Mr. Anderson to the church where he confessed Jests as his Lord and savior. He was baptized and the judge and congregation took communion with Him. Mrs. Anderson followed his example and was baptized. His sentence was commuted to life imprisonment. Later it was heard that Mr. Anderson was paroled.

Thoughts for the Week

Blessed assurance, Jesus is mine!
O what a fore taste of glory divine!
Heir of salvation, purchase of God,
born of his spirit, washed in his blood.

Perfect submission, perfect delight,
Visions of rapture burst on my sight:
angels descending bring from above
echoes of mercy, whispers of love.

Perfect submission, all is at rest
I in my savior am happy and blest,
watching and waiting, looking above,
filled with His goodness, lost in His love.

This is my story, this is my song,
praising my savior all the days long;
this is my story, this is my song,
praising my savior, all the days long.

Fanny Crosby, 1873

Prayer

Spirit of the living God, fall afresh on me.
Spirit of the living God, fall afresh on me.
Melt me, mold me, make me, and fill me.
Spirit of the living god, fall afresh on me,
David Iverson, 1926(Acts 11L 15)

O let the Son of God enfold you with his Spirit and his love.
Let him fill your heart and satisfy your soul.
O let him have the things that hold you, and his Spirit like a dove

will descend upon your life and make it whole.

Jesus, O Jesus, come and fill your lambs.
Jesus, O Jesus, come and fill your lambs.

John Wimber, 1979

Children

Scripture

1 A good man is to be more desired than great wealth. Favor is better than silver and gold.
2 The rich and the poor have a common bond; The Lord is the maker of them all.
3 The prudent sees the evil and hides himself, But the naive go on and are punished for it.
4 The reward of humility and the fear of the Lord are riches, honor and life.
5 Thorns and snares are in the way of the perverse; He who guards himself will be far from them.
6 Train up a child in the way he should go; even when he is old he will not depart from it.
Proverbs 22 1 - 6

17 "But when he came to his senses he said, "How many of my father's hired men have more than enough bred, but I am dying with hunger!
18 "I will get up and go to my father and will say to him, "Father, I have sinned against heaven, and in your sight;
19 I am no longer worthy to be called your son; make me one of your hired men."
20 "So he got up and came to his father. But when he was still a long way off, his father saw him and had compassion for him and ran and ran and embraced him and kissed him.
21 "And the son said to him. "Father I have sinned against heaven and in your sight, I and no longer worthy to be called your son."
22 "But his father said to his slaves, "Quickly, bring out the best rove and put it on him, and put a ring on his hand and sandals on his feet;
23 and bring the fattened calf, kill it and let us eat and celebrate:
24 for the son of mine was dead and has come to life again; and was lost and has been found." And they began to celebrate.
Luke 15: 17 - 24

4 Love is patient, love is kind and is not jealous; love does not brag and is not arrogant,
5 love is mot act unbecomingly; does not seek its own, is not provoked, does not take in to account a wrong suffered,
6 does not rejoice in unrighteousness, but rejoices with the truth,
7 bears all things, believes all things, knows all things, bears all things.
8 Love never fails; but if there are gifts of prophecy, they will be done away; if there are tongues, they will
cease; if there is knowledge it shall be done away.
9 For we know in part and we prophesy in part.
10 but when the perfect comes, the partial will be done away.
11 When I was a child, I used to speak like a child, think like a child, reason like a child,; when I became a man
I did away with childish things.
1 Corinthians 13: 4 -11

Meditation

Raising children is a God given privilege. Raising children is almost analogous to raising a garden. First, we plan and prepare the growing bed. We remove weeds and any noxious substances that might interfere with growth. For the best chance for the young, tender, newborns body and brain, you need mother with father's help, eliminate all harmful chemicals and nourish it with the best and appropriate diet and rest. To insure young and healthy plants we furnish them with clean water and appropriate nutrients.

When parents live calm, peaceful and loving life, the newborn infant has the best chance to relax and develop into a peaceful child with a calm, peaceful and loving body, mind and spirit. Where there is discord, anger and tension the infant becomes tense anxious and frightened. When the mother smokes marijuana or tobacco or other addicting drugs or excess alcohol, the fetus absorbs the chemicals and becomes addicted and may have neurological damage. When these infants are born they may exhibit the effects of these drugs and have to go through a period of withdrawal. With our example, help and advice, young parents can live a happy, healthy life and give their children a healthy, happy development.

It is a God given instinct for parents to develop a bond with their newborn infants. Bonding is an intense attachment that develops between parents and their baby. Bonding makes parents want to shower their little ones with love and affection and to protect and nourish them. The strong bond between parent and child provides the infant's mind for intimate relationship and fosters a sense of security and self-esteem. Parent's responsiveness to their infant's signals effects the child's social and cognitive development. The bond between the parent and child sets the stage for the child's mental and spiritual behavior for the rest of its life.

Train up a child in the way he should go, even when he is old he will not depart from it. (Proverbs22: 6) Tell a child that he is king and treat him like a king and he will grow up to be a king. Tell a child that he is good and treat it as a good child and it will usually grow up to be a good person. Tell a child that it is bad and it will be bad. Tell a child that it is a Muslim and treat it as a Muslim it will grow up thinking like a Muslim. Teach a child that it is a Hindu or Buddhist and it will grow up to think like a Hindu or Buddhist. Teach a child to be a Christian of Jew and act like a Christian or a Jew in its presence and it will grow up to think lid a Christian or Jew. Action speaks louder than words. Children will usually do what their parents, family and friends do. May we set good examples for our children as well as everyone that comes in contact with us.

Thoughts for the Week

Happy is the home when God is there,
and love fills every breast, when one their wish, and
one their prayer, and one their heavenly rest.

Happy is the home where Jesus' name
is sweet to every ear, where children early
speak his fame, and parents hold him dear.

Happy is the home where prayer is heard,
and praise is wont to rise, where parents love the
sacred word and all its wisdom prize.

Lord, let us in our homes agree
this blessed peace to gain; unite our hearts in
love to thee, and love to all will rise.
Henry Ware, 1840

Prayer

Dear Lord and Father of all man, kind, thank You for coming
down in the Christ Child. We stand in Awe as we read of your
growth into the Christ. We glory in the example You set for us
to see and follow as we grow in our love and fellowship with all
of Your children. May we as parents live a life that will shine as
a beacon for our children to follow. Let it shine for all to see and
guide them to Your love and life.
Amen

Childlike Faith

Scripture

13 Then some children were brought to Him so that He might lay
His hands of them and pray; and the disciples rebuked them.
14 But Jesus said, "Let the children com unto me, and do not
hinder them from coming to me; for the kingdom of heaven
belongs to such as these."
Matthew 19: 13, 14

1 At the same time the disciples came to Jesus and said, "Who then
is greatest in the kingdom of heaven?"
2 And He called a child to Himself and set him before them.
3 And said, "Truly I say to you, unless you and converted and
become like children, you will not enter the kingdom of heaven."
4 Whoever humbles himself as this child, he if the greatest in the
kingdom of heaven.
5 "And whoever receives one such child in My name receives Me.
6 And whoever causes one of these little ones who believe in Me
to stumble, it is better for him to have a millstone hung around his
neck, and to be drowned in the depth of the sea."
Matthew 18: 1 - 6

7 Jesus said to them again, "Truly, truly, I way to you, I am the
door of the sheep.
8 "any who came before Me are thieves and robbers, but the sheep
did not hear them.
9 "I am the door; if anyone enters through Me he will be saved,
and will go in and out and will find pasture.
10 "The thief comes only to steal and to kill and to destroy, I came
that they may have life, and have it abundantly."
11 "I am the good shepherd; the good shepherd lays down His life
for the sheep."
John 10: 7 - 11

Meditation

Blessed are the newborn babies. The newborn's mind is like a blank page, except instinctual movements that God sent with them for survival. The newborns are totally dependent of the mother or caregiver for the basic necessities of life and for the beginning foundation for trust relations with those in its world. As with lower animals, God gave us parenting desires for the growth and development of our little ones until they are able to provide for themselves and develop their own bodies, minds relationships and spiritual beliefs, and are able to leave the nest and care for themselves

Dr. Diane Komp is a Pediatric Oncologist. Her almost nonexistent faith in God slipped away until she could no longer believe in God. Dr. Komp writes, "If I were to believe, it would require the testimony of reliable witnesses." Her 'reliable witnesses' appeared in the lives of the suffering children she treated; children like Anna who developed enough energy to sit up in the bed and say, "Mamma, can you see them, the angels? Do you hear them singing?" Or her dying children and their parents also bore witness to God who restores life even in the face of death. She tells of parents who were angry enough to hate God but never lost faith. My own vision of God is more influenced by these parental theologians," writes Dr. Komp.

The disciples came to Christ and said, "Who then is the greatest in the kingdom of heaven?" And he called a child to Himself and set it before them, and said, "Truly I say to you, unless you are converted and become like children you will not enter the kingdom of heaven." Children who have been brought up to have faith in God and Jesus are innocent and pure. They have not been contaminated with the sins of self-righteousness, pride, greed and lust. They have not been soiled by the sins of guilt and have not developed the fear of death. Most children facing death are not unduly frightened and are more concerned with the parents' fear of losing them than their own dying.

Many children as they prepare to leave this life experience have a presence of childlike spirit, angels or a warm sense of impending peace. Some older persons who have a simple, childlike faith, experience visions and feelings and sense of peace.

Arnie Bryant was a young adolescent who was born with cerebral palsy and had little use of his arms or legs. He was taken care of by his father and sisters. He was seen in the emergency room one day deeply blue and barely breathing. He had a tracheotomy and admitted to ICU. He was sent home on a home aspirator. One day he told his daddy to call his sister. He told his daddy, "never mind, she is coming." His sister had the feeling that she had to go home. After she was with him a little while, she kissed him on his dimple and said she was giving him all the love that she had. He opened his eyes, smiled and closed them. She said she looked at his body but he was not there. She saw something with wings float up in the air and disappear.

Jesus said, "Whoever then humbles himself as a child, he is the greatest in the kingdom of heaven. And whoever receives one such child in My name receives Me."

Thoughts for the Week

Children of the heavenly Father in his bosom gather;
nestling bird nor star in heaven such a refuge e'er was given.

God his own doth tend and nourish in his holy courts they flourish;
from all evil he spares them; in his mighty arms he bears them.

Neither life nor death shall from them the Lord his children sever;
unto them his grace he showeth, and all their sorrows he knoweth

Though he giveth or he taketh, God his children ne'er forsaketh;
his the loving purpose solely to preserve them pure and holy.
Caroline V.Sandell-Berg, 11833

Prayer

All wise and loving heavenly Father, we are grateful
for our birth and the birth of our children and grandchildren.
Grant that we and our children continue to have childlike faith
until we are with You in heaven for eternity.
Amen

The Kingdom of Heaven

Scripture

17 From that time Jesus began to preach and say, "Repent, the kingdom of heaven is at hand."
20 Now having been questioned by the Pharisees to when the kingdom of God is coming, He answered them and said, "The kingdom of God is coming with signs to be observed;
21 nor will they say, "Look, here it is!" Or "There it is!" For behold, the kingdom is in your mist."
Luke 17: 20, 21

33 Then Pilot returned to the praetorian and summoned Jesus and said to Him, "Are you the king of the Jews?"
34 Jesus answered, "Are you saying this on your own initiative, or did others tell you about Me?"
35 Pilot answered Him, "I am not a Jew, am I? Your own nation and the chief priests delivered You to me; what have You done?"
36 Jesus answered, "My kingdom is not of this world. If My kingdom were of this world then My servants would be fighting so that I would not be handed over to the Jew; but as it is, My kingdom is not of this realm."
John 18:33 - 36

14 I know and am convinced in the Lord Jesus that nothing is unclean in itself; but to him who thinks anything to be unclean, to him it is unclear.
15 For if because food your brother is hurt, you are not walking according to love Do not destroy with your food him for whom Christ died.
16 Therefore do not let what is for you a good thing be spoken of as evil;
17 for the kingdom of God in not eating and drinking, but righteousness and peace and joy in the Holy Spirit.
Romans 4: 14 - 17

Meditation

For a child will be born to us and will be given to us; and the government will rest upon His shoulders; and His name will be called Wonderful, Counselor, Mighty God, Eternal Father, Prince of Peace. There will be no end to the increase of His government or of peace; on the throne of David over the kingdom to establish it and to uphold it with justice and righteousness. Isaiah 9: 6, 7

The Hebrew people believed that the child would be born to be king of the Jews and sit on the throne of David and rule with peace and righteousness King Herod believed that Jesus would grow up, overthrow him and become a military leader of Israel. He tried to have Jesus killed.

And the word became flesh and dwelt among us, and we saw His glory, glory of the only begotten Son from the Father, full of grace and truth. John testified about Him and cried out saying, "This is He of whom I said He who comes after me has a higher rank than I, for He existed before me. "

As soon as He was alone, His followers, along with the twelve began asking Him about the parables. And He was saying to them, "To you have been given the mysteries of the kingdom of God. But those outside get everything in parables so that while seeing, they may see and not perceive, otherwise they might return and be forgiven. Mark 4: 10 -12

Jesus taught that the kingdom of God, kingdom of heaven was in the mind and among those who believe in Him and his Father and follow His examples of truth and love. In the parable of sowing seeds, the seed was the word and the sower was the word of God or His followers who spread the word. The word falls on some who refuse to listen and receive the work. The word falls on some who listen but their belief is shallow so that they quickly slip back into their usual sinful ways. On some, the work falls, takes roots and grows. Through them the word is spread to others. Like a tiny mustard seed grows into a large plant, their word spreads to others and the kingdom grows into a large crowd of believers.

Thoughts for the Week

The kingdom of God is like a grain of mustard seed.
When it is sown in the earth, it is the smallest seed.
It is the kingdom of God and is a mystery.

For when it is sown, it grows into the largest plant,
greater than all the herbs, and grows into a tree.
It is the kingdom of God and is a mystery.

It grows so that birds can rest inside its crown of leaves,
deep in its shadows, away from any evil pray.
It is the kingdom of God and is a mystery.

And we can liken it to seed which make a tree
larger than all the trees from just the smallest seed.
It is the kingdom of God and a mystery.
Gracia Grindal , 1983

Prayer

We've a story to tell to the nation,
that turn their hearts to the right,
a story of truth and mercy, a story of
peace and light, a story of peace and light.

We've a song to sing to the nations,
that shall lift their hearts to the Lord,
a song that shall conquer evil and shatter the
spear and sword, and shatter the spear and sword.

We've a message to give to the nations,
that the Lord who reigneth above hath sent His Son to save us,
and show us that God is Love, and show us that God is Love.

We've a Savior to show to the nations,
who the path of sorrow hath trod,
That all of the world's great peoples might come to the
truth of God, might come to the truth of God.
H. Ernest Nichol, 1892

Angels

Scripture

10 Abraham stretched out his hand and took the knife to slay his son.
11 But the angel of the Lord called to him from heaven and said, "Abraham, Abraham! And he said, "Here I am."
12 He said, "Do not stretch out your hand against the lad, and do nothing to him; for now I know that you fear God, since you have not withheld your son, your only son, from, Me."
Genesis 2: 10 - 12

26 Now in the sixth month the angel Gabriel was sent to a city in Galilee named Nazareth,
27 to a virgin engaged to a man whose name was Joseph of the descendants of David; and the virgins name was Mary.
28 And coming in he said to her, "Greetings, favored one! The Lord is with you."
29 But she was very perplexed at the statement and kept pondering what kind of statement this was.
30 The angel said to her, "Do not be afraid, Mary; for you have found favor with God.
31 "And behold, you will conceive in your womb and bear a son and you shall name Him Jesus."
Luke 2: 26 - 31

8 In the region there were shepherds staying out in the fields and keeping watch over their flock
9 by night... And an angel of the Lord stood before them, and the glory of the Lord shone around them, and they were terribly frightened.
10 But the angel said to them, "Do not be afraid, for behold, I bring you good news which will be of great joy which will be for all the people;
11 for today in the city of David there have been born for you a Savior, who is Christ the Lord.

12 "This will be a sign for you: you will find a baby wrapped in cloths lying in a manger.

13 And suddenly there appeared with them the angel a multitude of heavenly host praising God and saying.

14 "Glory to God in the highest. And on earth peace among men with whom He is Pleased."

Luke 2; 8 -14

1 Now after the Sabbath, as it began to dawn toward the first day of the week Mary Magdalene and the other Mary came to look at the grave.

2 And behold, a severe earthquake had occurred for an angel of the Lord descended from heaven and came and rolled away the stone and sat upon it.

3 And his appearance was like lightening and his clothing was as snow.

4 The guards shook for fear of him and became like dead men.

5 The angel said to the women, "Do not be afraid; for I know that you are looking for Jesus who has been crucified.

6 "He is not here, for He has risen, just as He said, come and see the place where He was lying."

Matthew 28: 1 - 6

Meditation

Angels have been seen by and believed in by Christianity, Judaism, Islam, and other religions as an intermediary between heaven and earth and a spiritual messenger of God. God tested Abraham when Abraham believed that God wanted him to offer his only son, Isaac, as a burnt offering to Him to show his obedience and fear of Him Abraham stretched out his hand to take his knife and slay his son. But the angel of the Lord called to him from heaven and said, "Abraham, Abraham!" And he said, "Here I am." And he said, "Do not stretch out your hand against the lad, and do nothing to him. For now I know that you fear God, since you have not withheld your son, your only son from me. Genesis 23: 10 - 12

Angels have appeared to man since the beginning of man. God sent a Cherub in to guard the way to the tree life after the fall of man. The angel Gabriel appeared to Zacharias and informed him that his wife, Elizabeth, would bear a child, John, who would be the forerunner before the Messiah. An angel appeared to Joseph in a dream and told him to take the child Egypt because King Herod was going to search for the child and destroy Him. He will give his angels charge to guard you in all your ways. They will bear you up in their hands, that you do not strike your foot against a stone. Psalms 91: 11, 12

Dr. Diane Komp, a Pediatric Oncologist, relates stories on children with leukemia and other fatal illnesses. She tells of Anna, who was treated for leukemia for five years before she faced the end of her life at the age of seven. Before she died she sat up in bed and said, "The angels, they are so beautiful! Mamma, do you see them? Do you hear them singing? I've never heard such beautiful singing!" Then she lay back on her pillow and died.

There was a four old Asian boy whose family did not practice a Christian faith, which had a vision of angels visiting him and summoned members of the hospital staff into his room. He thanked each of them for helping him and they said, "Goodbye." He lay down and died. He was not upset, not in the least.

Tom was nineteen when his cancer recurred, but he refused to accept the relapse as a death sentence. When Dr. Komp visited him he could not move his legs nor lift his arms. When they were alone he told Dr. Komp of a vision that came to him when he was meditation. Tom saw himself in a beautiful garden and saw a man there, seated on a bench. The man walked with him in the garden and talked to him. The man touched him, and Tom reported that he moved in the bed for the first time in months. Tom did not want to leave the garden nor the man's presence. Dr. Komp asked Tom if he knew who the man was. He said, "I know that it was Jesus."

A colleague of Dr. Komp told her of an eight year old boy with cancer whose parents did not like discussing matters of death or matters of faith despite obvious signs that their son would die within a few days. The boy took them by surprise one morning with the report of a dream. A big yellow school bus pulled up to the house in his dream and the door opened. On the bus, he saw Jesus, who told him of his impending death and invited him to go with Him on the bus. It was with great peace that he accepted Jesus' invitation as he recounted his dream to his parent.

We had a maid several years ago who had a son with advanced prostate cancer and had a lot of bone pain. He had a brother and sister who had died in early childhood. He told his mother that when the image of his brother and sister were at his bedside, he had no pain at all. Many have angels, visions or spirits as they have problems and when they prepare to leave this life on earth.

Thoughts for the Week

I come to the garden alone while the dew is still on the roses,
and the voice I hear falling on my ear the Son of God discloses.
And he walks with me, and he talks with me, and he tells me that I am his own;
and the joy we share as we tarry there, none other has ever known

He speaks, and the sound of his voice is so sweet the birds hush their singing,
and the melody he gave to me within my heart is ringing.
And he walks with me, and he talks with me, and he tells me that I am his own,
and the joy we share as we tarry there, none other has ever known

I'd stay in the garden with him though the night around me be falling,
but he bids me go; thru the voice of woe his voice to me is calling.
And he walks with me and he talks with me,
and he tells me that I am dis own;
and the joys we share as we tarry there, none other has ever known.
C. Austin Miles, 1913

Prayer

Almighty, ever loving and everlasting Father, we praise you and thank you for sending your angelic messengers for our comfort and peace. May we and our little ones join you and the heavenly house when we leave this earthly home.
Amen

God's Desire for Man

Scripture

15 The Lord God took the man and put him into the Garden of Eden to cultivate it and keep it.
16 The Lord God commanded the man, saying, "From any tree in the garden you may eat freely;
17 but from the tree of the knowledge of good and evil you shall not eat, for in the day that you eat it you will surely die."
Genesis 2: 15 - 17

17 Every good thing given and every perfect gift is from above, coming down from the Father of light, with whom there is no variation or shifting shadow.
18 In the exercises of His will he brought us forth by the word of truth, so that we would be a kind of first fruit among His creatures.
19 This you know, my beloved brethren. But everyone must be quick to hear, slow to speak and slow to anger,
20 for the anger of man does not achieve the righteousness of God.
James 1: 17 - 20

Meditation

In the beginning, God placed man in the Garden of Eden to cultivate it and keep it. God's intentional desire was for man to have everything to sustain him and to enjoy life in peace.

However, Adam and Eve disobeyed God and took of the tree of good and evil, so they had to toil and strain for survival and had to work to obtain peace. The descendants of Adam became corrupt in the site of God and the world was filled with violence, except for Noah. "Go out of the ark, you and your wife and your sons' wives with you. Bring with you every living thing of all flesh that is with you. Birds and animal, and every living thing that creeps on the earth, which they may breed abundantly on the earth and be

beautiful and multiply on the earth."
Genesis 19: 16, 17

For many years the Hebrews struggled for freedom and peace to live in a Hebrew nation. It was a constant struggle to gain and regain freedom in a Hebrew nation. During the struggle against Roman domination many Jews were killed and there was large expulsion of the Jewish population. In the seventh century, the Byzantine Empire conducted a massacre and expulsion of the Jews.

It was not God's will for man to struggle, fight and hate others but instead for all mankind to live in peace and love and brotherhood. God knew the evil ways of man and came down in the person of Jesus the Christ to show and teach man how to live in peace and to have respect and love for their neighbors. It continues to be God's desire for man to live in peace and harmony. God's desire was always for all people to live in peace, love and harmony. Other people in the world have their own beliefs of God and brotherhood.

Islam meant peace, dedication and obedience. There are groups of people in every religion that deviate from the true meaning of their religion. The Qur'an tells the Muslims to take care of widows and orphans. Modern Buddhist teaches offers a spiritual path for cultivating inner calm, clarity, and strength; a healing methodology to bring assistance to those undergoing illness and other hardships; and a positive voice that will benefit humanity as a whole.

Hinduism believes in the existence of a supreme being, the creator of the universe. The Supreme Being or God is the supreme soul. They believe in individual freedom to believe and there is no such thing as hearsay, which does not exist. Hindus believes that God's desire for them is to live daily morality, respect for others and respect for the earth and all of God's creatures.

Native American religion is closely connected to the land in which Native Americans live and the spiritual. Native American religions tend to be carried out mainly in a family and tribal relation first and are explained as a process or journey rather than a religion.

There is a relationship between Creator and created. For Native Americans, religion is never separated from one's daily life. For Native Americans, a relationship with God is experienced as a relationship with all creation, which is ever present and does not require an institution of building. To them, God is the Great Spirit, Creator or Sky Chief. When the Great Spirit ties a brave to his princes together they walk life's path together for the rest of their lives. The Native Americans concern is truth and love for members of the tribe and family.

Thoughts for the Week

The Great Father above a Shepherd Chief is.
I am His and with Him I want not.
He throws out to me a rope
and the name of the rope is love
and He draws me to where the grass is green
and the Water is not dangerous,
And eat and lie down and am satisfied.
Sometime my heart is very weak and falls down
but He lifts me up again and draws me into a good road
His name is Wonderful.

Sometime, it may be very soon, it may be a long m long time,
He will draw me into a valley.
It will be dark, but I'll be afraid not,
for it is between those mountains
that the Shepherd Chief will meet me
and the hunger that I have in my heart all through life
will be satisfied.

Sometimes he makes the love rope into a whip,
but afterwards He gives me a staff to lean upon.
He spreads a table before me with all kinds of foods,
He puts His hand upon my head and all the "thirst" is gone

My cup he fills till it runs over.
What I tell is true.
I lie not.
These roads that are" away ahead" will stay with me
through this life and after;
and afterwards I will go to live in the Big Teepee
and sit down with the Shepherd Chief forever.
George Hunt

Prayer

Our Father who dwells on High
Good for our hearts Your Name.
Good you Chief of all people;
Good Your heart to make our country such as Yours
Give us all day our food.
And stop remembering all our sins we make to them,
As we suppose their sins against us;
Throw away from us all evil.
Amen
Kloshe Kahkwa

Saint Georgia

Scripture

15 So when they had finished breakfast. Jesus said to Simon Peter, son Of John, "Do you love me more than these? He said to him, "Yes Lord, You know that I love You" He said to him, "Tend My lambs."
16 He said to him a second time, "Simon, son of John, do you love Me?" He said to Him, "yes Lord, You Know that I love You." He said to him, "Shepherd My Sheep."
17 He said to him a third time, "Simon, son of John, do you love me?" Peter was grieved because He said to him the third time, "Do you love Me?" And the said to Him Lord, You know all things, You know that I love You." Jesus said to him, "Tend My sheep."
John 21: 15 - 17

34 Then the king will say to those on His right, "Come, you who are blessed of My Father, inherit the kingdom prepared for you since the foundation of the world.
35 For I was hungry and you gave Me something to eat; I was thirsty and you gave Me something to drink; I was a stranger and you invited Me in;
36 naked and you clothed Me; I was sick and you visited Me; I was in prison and you came to Me."
37 Then the righteous will answer Him, "Lord, when did we see You hungry and feed You. Or thirsty and gave you something to drink?
38 "and when did we see You a stranger, and invite you in, or naked and cloth You?
39 "When did we see You sick, or in prison, and come to You?"
40 The King will answer and say to them, "Truly I say to you, "to the extent that you did it to one of these brothers of mine, even the least of them, you did it to Me."
Matthew 25: 34 - 40

Meditation

Years ago, Georgia was born into a poor family in the country. When she was young, she took Jesus into her life, studied the bible and always tried to obey His word. She loved Christ and everything that she came in contact with. She worked as a maid for several families. Our family hired her as a part time maid. Every time a baby was born, Georgia was quick to visit the family and offer to help take care of the mother and newborn. When our children arrived, she helped take care of them. She loved each of them and they also loved her. When one of our young ones was entered in pre-kindergarten, she cried until we had to take her home because she loved Georgia so and did not want to leave her.

When she knew that someone was sick, she visited them and helped take care of them. When she heard of someone in jail, she visited them and witnessed to them. She was always at the church when someone died. She was a deaconess and was always in front of the church with the family mourning with them and comforting them. As Jesus said, "For whoever wished to save his life will lose it, but whoever loses his life for My sake and the gospel's will save it. For what does it profit a man to gain the whole world and forfeit his soul?" Mark 9: 5

There are many other saintly people who have saved their lives by losing their lives for Christ and the gospel. David Livingstone gave his life for Christ and the gospel as the spread the word throughout Africa. Mother Theresa gave her life to minister to the poorest of the poor in India. Brother Bryant gave his life to minister to the poor, cold and hungry of Birmingham, Alabama. Charles Pitman tells of Bill Yopp, a southern slave, who gave his life to minister to his master, the injured confederate and Yankee soldiers and every one he served, in his book, Ten Cent Bill. Abraham Lincoln gave his life to free the slaves in America and to abolish slavery. There are many other others, like Saint Georgia, who have saved their lives by serving Christ.

Thoughts for the Week

Take my life and let it be, consecrated, Lord, to Thee.
Take my moments and my days; let them flow in ceaseless praise.
Take my hands, and let them move at the impulse of thy love
Take my feet and let them be swift and beautiful for thee.

Take my voice and let it sing always only, for my king.
Take my lips and let them be filled with messages from thee.
Take my silver and my gold; not a mite would I withhold.
Take my intellect, and use every power as thou shalt choose

Take my will and make it thine; it shall be no longer mine.
Take my heart, it is thine own; it shall be thy royal throne.
Take my love, my Lord; I pour at thy feet its treasure store.
Take myself, and I will ever be ever, only, for thee.
Frances R. Havergal, 1873

Prayer

Lord, help me live from day to day
In such a self-forgetful way,
That when I kneel to pray,
My prayer shall be for "others"

Help me in all the work I do
To ever be sincere and true,
And know that all I do for you
Must need be done foe "others."

And when my work on earth is done,
And my new work in heaven's begun,
Ma I forget the crown I've won.
While thinking still of "others"

"Others, Lord. Yes, "others"
Let this my motto be,

Help me to live for others
That I may live like Thee.
The Prayer, "Others"

Priorities

Scripture

6 With what shall I cone to the Lord and bow myself before the God on high? Shall I come to Him with burnt offerings, with yearling calves?
7 Does the Lord take delight in thousands of rams, in ten thousand rivers of oil? Shall I present my firstborn for my rebellious sins, the fruit of my body for the sin of my soul?
8 He has told you O man, what is good, and what the Lord requires of you but to do justice, to love kindness, and to walk humbly with your God.
Micah 6: 6 - 8

18 A ruler questioned Him, saying, "Good teacher, what shall I do to inherit eternal life?"
19 And Jesus said to him, "Why do you call Me good? No one is good except God alone.
20 You know the Commandments, "Do not commit adultery, do not murder, do not steal, do not bear false
witness, honor your father and mother."
21 And he said, "All these things I have kept from my youth."
22 When Jesus heard this, He said to him, "One thing you still lack; Sell all that you possess and distribute it to the poor, and you shall have treasures in heaven; and come, follow Me."
Luke 18: 18 - 22

Meditation

When we were babies, we were totally dependent on our families. We had no concept of pride, greed, hatred or concept of self. As we matured, we developed greed, anger, pride, love, and desires that our families and society taught, by word, example, and deed. At an early age, we were taught what to believe and what was important in life and established our priorities.

As Christians, we were taught to believe in God, Jesus, love, and respect for others and all of God's creatures. Some believed strongly in what they felt to be most important. So, we developed different religions, denominations, churches, and sects. Each denomination or sect taught what they believed to be necessary for life and for salvation.

The Jewish faith believed that there were certain aspects of a godly life that insured salvation and the existence of a Hebrew nation and to stay in favor of God. The Hindu set priorities for living in peace with man and all of God's creatures. Buddhism has its own priorities. The Muslim religion teaches to care for all that believe as they do. They also believe that they should destroy their enemies. Muslims believe that if they die in battle with unbelievers, they will be rewarded in paradise.

Jesus taught that we should love our enemies. Jesus said, "You have heard it said, you shall love your neighbor and hate your enemy, But I say to you, love your enemy and pray for those who persecute you, so that you might be the sons of your Father who is in heaven; for He causes His son to rise on the evil and the good, and sends rain on the righteous and the unrighteous." Matthew 5: 43 - 45

As young children, we learned to live as our families, forefathers and friends lived. As we matured, we continued to live and believe as we were taught or rebelled and developed our own priorities. Some developed pride, greed, hatred, and a desire to develop worldly goods, social status and financial success. Celebrity, pride and power may be more important than humility of love for our neighbors. We may change our priorities due to some life threatening events, by examples of others or guidance of a mentor.

The apostle Peter said, "And now brethren, I know that you acted in ignorance, just as your ruler also. But the things God announced before by the mouth of the prophets, that His Christ would suffer. He has thus fulfilled. Therefore repent and return, as that your sins may be wiped away, in order that times of refreshing

may come, from the presence of the Lord.
Luke 2: 127 - 19

Thoughts for the Week

'Twas battered and scarred, and the auctioneer
Thought it scarcely worth his while
To spend much time on the old violin
But he held it up with a smile

"What am I bidden for this?" he cried
"Who'll start the bidding for me?"
A dollar...one dollar; then two...only two:
Two dollars are bidden; say three.

"Three dollars once: Three dollars twice:
Going for three!" But lo!
From the back of the crowd a grey-haired man
Came forward and picked up the bow

Then, wiping the dust from the old violin
And tight'ning the loosened strings
He played a melody passing sweet
The kind that haunts and clings

The music ceased, and the auctioneer
With a voice that was soft and low
Said, "Now what is bid for the old violin?"
And he held it up with the bow.

"A thousand dollars: Who'll make it two?"
Two...two thousand; say three!
Three thousand once, three thousand twice,
Three thousand...gone!" said he

The people cheered, but some exclaimed
"We do not quite understand...

What changed its worth?" and the answer came:
'Twas the touch of the master's hand."

And many a man with soul out of tune
And battered and scarred by sin
Is auctioned cheap by the thoughtless crowd
Just like the old violin

But the Master comes, and the foolish crowd
Never can quite understand
The worth of a soul, and the change that is wrought
By the touch of the master's hand

O Master! I am the tuneless one
Lay, lay Thy hand on me
Transform me now; put a song in my heart
Of melody, Lord, to Thee!

Myra B Welch

Prayer

Out of the depths I cry to you; O Lord, now hear me calling.
Incline your ear to my distress in spite of my rebelling.
Do not regard my sinful deeds.
Send me the grace my spirit needs;
Without it I am nothing.

All things you send are full of grace; you crown our lives with
favor.
All our good works are done in vain without our Lord and Savior.
We praise the God who gives us faith and saves us from the
gro of death; our lives are in God's keeping

It is in God that we shall hope; and not in our own merit;
We rest our faith in god's good word
and trust the Holy Spirit, whose promise keeps us
strong and sure; we trust the Holy

signature inscribed upon our temple.

My soul is waiting for the Lord as one whom
longs for morning; no watcher waits with greater hope
then I for Christ's returning. I hope as Israel
in the Lord, who sends redemption
through the word. Praise God for endless mercy.
Martin Luther, 1523

Thanksgiving

Scripture

8 Oh give thanks to the Lord, call upon His name. Make known His deeds among the peoples.
9 Sing to Him, sing praises to His name; Speak of all His wonders.
10 Glory in His holy name; Let the heart of those who see the Lord be glad.
1 Chronicles 16: 8 -10

1 Give thanks to the Lord, for He is good. For His loving kindness is everlasting.
2 Give thanks to the Lord of gods, for His loving kindness is everlasting.
3 Give thanks to the Lord of lords, for his loving kindness is everlasting;
4 To Him who alone does greets wonders, for His loving kindness is everlasting;
5 To Him who made the heavens with skill, for His loving kindness is everlasting;
6 To Him who spread out the earth above the waters, for His loving kindness is everlasting;
7 To Him who made the great lights, for His loving kindness is everlasting:
8 The sun to rule by day, for his loving kindness is everlasting;
9 The moon and stars to rule by night, for His loving kindness is everlasting.
Psalm 136: 1 - 9

34 And Jesus said to them, "How many loves do you have?" And they said, "Seven and a few small fishes."
35 And He directed the people to sit on the ground;
36 And He took the seven loves and the fishes and giving thanks, He broke them and started giving them to the disciples, and the disciples gave them to the people.

37 And they all ate and were satisfied, and they picked up what was left over of the broken pieces, seven large baskets full.
Matt hew 15: 34 - 37

7 Sing to the Lord with thanksgiving; Sing to our God on the lyre,
8 who cover the heavens with clouds, who provides rain for the earth, who makes grasses to grow on the mountains.
9 He gives to the beast its food, and to the young ravens who cry
Psalm 147: 7 - 9

Meditation

The pilgrims settled the Plymouth Colony in 1620. By the grace of God and the help of friendly Indians, they had shelter and food to last through the first winter. The nest year they had a good harvest and wild game in store for the next winter. The pilgrims set apart a day the next November as a harvest festival.

William Bradford of Plymouth Plantation said, "They began to gather in the small harvest they had and to fill up the houses and dwellings against winter, being all recovered in health and strength and had all things in good plenty. For some were thus employed in affairs abroad, others were exercised in fishing, about Cod and bass and other fish, of which they took good store, of which every family had their portion. All the summer there was no want, and now began to store of foul as winter approached, of which this place did abound when they came first(but afterward decreased by degree). And besides there were great store of wild turkey of which they took many, besides venison, etc. Besides they had abundant supplies and a peck of meal a week per person harvest, Indian corn to the proportion. This made many afterward write so largely of their plenty here to their friends in England. Which were not frightened by the report?" The Continental Congress pronounced a day of thanksgiving in December in 1777 and 1783. The proclamation of President George Washington, in 1789 proclaimed November 16, 1789 to be a national day of thanksgiving. President Abraham Lincoln, prompted by a series of editorials Sarah Joseph Hale, proclaimed a day of thanksgiving to be celebrated on the final Thursday 1863.

Thoughts for the Week

Come ye thankful people come, raise the song of harvest home;
all is gathered safely in, ere the winter storm begin.
God our maker doth provide for our wants to be supplied;
come to God's own temple, come, raise the song of harvest home.

All the world is God's own field; fruit as praise God will yield;
wheat and tares together sown are to joy or sorrow grown;
first the blade and then the ear, then the fill corn shall appear;
Lord of harvest, grant that we whole-some grain and pure may be.

For the Lord our God shall come, and shall take the harvest home;
for the field shall in that day all offences purge away,
giving angels charge at last in the fires the tares to cast;
but the fruitful ears to store in the garden ever more.

Even so, Lord, quickly come; bring thy final harvest home;
gather thou the people in, free from sorrow, free from sin,
there forever purified in thy presence to abide; come, with thine angels, come, raise the glorious harvest home.
Henry Alford, 1844

Prayer

God of love, we thank you for all for which you have
blessed us ever to this day:
for the gift of joy in days of health and strength,
And for the gifts of your abiding presence and promise

In days of pain and grief...
We praise you for home and friends,
and for our baptism and place in your church
and all who have lived and died.

Above all else we thank you for Jesus who knew our
grieves,
who died our death and rose for our sake,
and who lives and prays for us.
So as he taught us, so now we pray.
Amen
Service and worship of the United Methodist Church

Allegiance

Scripture

21 They questioned Him, saying, "Teacher, we know that You speak and teach correctly, and You are not partial to any, but teach the way of God in truth.
22 "Is it lawful for us to pay taxes to Caesar, or not?"
23 "Show Me a denarius, whose likeness and inscription does it have? They said, "Caesars."
25 And He said to them, "Then render to Caesar the things that are Caesar's and to God the things that are God's."
Luke 20: 21 - 25

16 Whenever you fast, do not put on a gloomy face as the hypocrites do for they neglect the appearance so that they will be noticed by men when they are fasting. Truly I say to you, they have their reward in full.
17 But you when you fast anoint your head and wash your face
18 so that your fasting will not be noticed by men, but by your Father who is in secret; and your Father who sees what is done in secret will reward you.
19 "Do not store up for your selves treasures on earth, where moth and rust destroys, and where thieves brake in and Steal.
20 "But store up for your selves treasures in heaven, where neither moth nor rust destroys, and where thieves do not break in or steal;
21 for where your treasure is there your heart will be also...
Matthew 6: 16 - 21

Meditation

After the crucifixion of Jesus, Peter and the other disciples began preaching to the people of the resurrection of Jesus and that Jesus was the Christ, the son of the living God. The Hebrew religious leader tried to stop Peter and the apostles from spreading the word. The followers continued to grow in number. Then Stephen pledged his allegiance to the word and was chosen to lead the people to follow the teachings of Jesus and do the will of God. Because of Stephens alliance with the teaching of the Christ, the religious leaders and those allegiant to the ways and beliefs of the existing Hebrew faith, had Stephen stoned to death.

Despite the persecution of those allegiant toes the teachings of Christ, the numbers continued to grow, the captain went along with the officers and proceeded to bring them back without violence. (for he was afraid of the people, that they might be stoned). When they had brought them, they stood them before the council. The high priest questioned them, saying, "We gave you strict orders not to continue teaching in this name, and yet you filled Jerusalem your teachings and intent to bring this man's blood upon us. But Peter and the apostles answered, "We must obey God rather that man. The God of our fathers raised up Jesus, whom you had put to death by hanging Him on a cross."   Acts 5: 26 -30

Through history man has had to choose what he believed to be true and right or what society said. During the Roman Empire, Christians had to continue to worship God and spread the word in secret or face persecution and death at the will of the Roman government. During the rise and fall of the Third Reich, Christians and Jews had to choose to profess the beliefs of the Nazi government or be persecuted and put to death. Christians, Jews, Hindu, and Muslims were sent to concentration camps and gas chambers if they did not pledge allegiance to the Nazi controlled government. German children were sent to Nazi controlled schools and taught to obey the state.

The United States was founded on a belief in God, freedom of religion, freedom of speech, human rights, and the right to worship as they pleased. Over the years the elected politicians have tried to remove God, Jesus, the Ten Commandments from public events and buildings. Schools have been legislated what they could and could not teach our children. It remains parent's right and pleasure to teach our children right from wrong, belief in God, love for others, love for God's earth, proper behavior, self-respect, and freedom to place their allegiance to what they believed to be right. Other churches such as the Russian Orthodox Church, Russian Catholic Church, other churches, religious groups, denominations, sects, and cults have demanded that people under their control pledge their allegiance to them. God gives each individual the right to pledge allegiance to whom he or she believes to be right.

Thoughts for the Week

O Lord, may church and home continue to teach the perfect way,
with gentleness and love like thin, that none shall ever stray.

Let all unworthy aim depart, imbue us with thy grace;
within the home let every heart become thy dwelling place.

Shine, Light divine; reveal thy face where darkness else might be.
Grant, love divine, in every place gladly fellowship with thee.

May steadfast faith and earnest prayer keep sacred vows secure;

build thou a hallowed dwelling where joy and peace
endure.
Carlton C, Buck, 1961

Prayer

O Master, let me walk with the in lowly paths of service
free; tell me thy secret;
help me bear the strain of toil, the fret of care.

Help me the slow of heart to move by some clear winning
word of love,
teach me the way to feet to stray, and guide them in the
homeward way.

Teach me thy patience; still with thee in closer, dearer
company,
in work that keeps faith sweet and strong, in trust that
triumphs over wrong;

In hope that sends a shining ray far down the further
broadening,
in peace that only thou can give, with thee, O Master, let
me live.
Washington Gladden, 1879,

Christmas

Scripture

6 For a child will be born to us, a son will be given to us;
and the government will rest upon His shoulders;
and His name will be called Wonderful, Counselor, Mighty
God. Eternal Father, Prince of peace.
7 There will be no end to the increase of His government or
of peace, On the throne of David and over His kingdom, to
establish it and to uphold it with justice and righteousness.
From then on and forevermore.
The zeal of the Lord of host will establish this.
Isaiah 9: 6,7

21 "She will bear a Son, and you shall call His name Jesus,
for He will save His people from their sins."
22 Now all this took plate to fulfill what was spoken by the
Lord through the prophets:
23 "Behold, THE VIRGIN SHALL BE WITH CHILD
AND SHALL BEAR A SON, AND THEY SHALL CALL
HIS NAME, "IMMANUEL." Which translated means,
"God with us"
Matthew : 21 - 23

26 Mow in the sixth month the angel Gabriel was sent from
God to a city in Galilee called Nazareth,
27 to a virgin engaged to a man whose name was Joseph, of
the descendants of David, and the virgin's name was Mary.
28 And coming in he said to her, "Greeting, favored one!
The Lord is with you.
29 But she was very perplexed at this statement, and kept
pondering what kind of salutation this was.
30 The angel said to her, "Do not be afraid, Mary, for you Have
found favor with God.
31 And behold, you will conceive in your womb and bear a son,
and you shall name Him Jesus.
32 "He will be great and He will be called the Son of the most

High; and the Lord God will give Him the throne of His Father David;

33 and He will reign over the house of Jacob forever, and His kingdom will have no end."

Luke 1: 26 - 33

8 In the same region there were some shepherds staying out in the field and keeping watch over their flock by night.

9 An angel of the Lord suddenly stood before them and the glory of the Lord shone around them; and they were terribly frightened.

10 But the angel said to them, "Do not be afraid; for behold, I bring you good news of great joy which will be for all the people;

11 for today in the city of David there has been born for you a Savior, who is Christ the Lord.

12 This will be a sign for you; you will find a baby wrapped in clothes and lying in a manger

13 And suddenly there appeared with them a multitude of heavenly host praising God and saying,

14 "Glory be to God in the highest, and on earth peace among men with whom He is Pleased."

Luke 2: 8 -14

Meditation

God's intentional will was for man live in peace and harmony but man chose to gain knowledge of good and evil. As man grew in number, the world was filled with hatred, lust and greed. So God chose to destroy man that He had created. He did know that Noah had been a faithful, God fearing, loving and honest man. God destroyed Man that he created except for Noah and his family. Noah's descendants through Abraham continued to be God fearing and peaceful people.

Because Sarah could not have children, Abraham had a son Ishmael by Sarah's maid, Hagar. After the birth of Isaac, Sarah did not want Ishmael to have her son's inheritance, so Ishmael was sent into Egypt and promised by God to raise a great nation. One of the descendants of Ishmael was Muhammad. For some time, the descendants of Isaac and Ishmael was friendly. After the enslavement of the Israelites by the Egyptians, the Muslims and Hebrews have been enemies and there have been wars between the Hebrew nation and the other nations, the people of Jericho, Syria, Babylon, and other non-Hebrew nations.

God came down in the spirit and mind on Jesus to show and teach the people the way of love, peace and brotherhood. His angels (messengers) appeared to Martha, John the Baptist, Mary and Joseph and shepherds in the fields proclaiming Jesus to be the Christ, Lord, Prince of peace, Immanuel (God with us). The birthday of Jesus, we now call, ""Christmas", some of the people In Israel believed in him and followed His life and teachings and His spirit and teaching ha spread around the world. Some religious leaders rejected Him and had Him killed by hanging on a cross.

Christmas has been celebrated by peace, love of neighbor and love of family. Children have been given gifts by the spirit of Christmas (Santa Claus), or whatever name given to him. Down through the ages we have drifted away from the meaning of Christmas.

Business people and merchants have used Christmas as a time to sell toys, and other gifts to raise money and seek wealth. Some of the most memorable and rewarding Christmases to children and adults alike have been when they found someone in need and ministered to them. The spirit of Christmas can be felt when a child is hungry and given something to eat. The spirit of Christmas can be felt when someone is found without shoes or warm clothing to wear hear their thanks and joy as we give them something warm to wear.

The spirit of Christmas can be felt when we find someone sick and visit and minister to them, the spirit of Christmas felt when we enjoy the love with our families and friends and when we sing praises to God for coming to show us the way of truth and love. Some peoples who were isolated from the routes of trade and wars were already living a life of love of family and neighbors or members of their tribe before Christ came. Some Native Americans, Hindu, followers of Buddha, and probably others lived in peace and harmony with their families and neighbors. May we all have a very merry Christmas as we remember the meaning of what Christ came to show and teach us.

Thoughts for the Week

Hark! The herald angels sang. "Glory to the newborn king; peace on earth and mercy mild, God and sinners reconciled." Joyful all ye nations rise, join the triumph of the skies; with the angelic host proclaim, "Christ is born in Bethlehem". Christ by highest heaven adored; Christ the everlasting Lord; Late in time behold him come, offspring of the virgin's womb. Veiled in flesh the God-head see; hail the incarnate Deity, pleased with us in flesh to dwell, Jesus, our Emanuel. Hail to heaven-born Prince of Peace! Hail the Sun of Righteousness! Light and life to all he brings, risen with healing in his wings. Mild he lays his glory by. Born that we no more may die, born to raise us from the earth, born to give us second birth Hark the herald angels sing, , "Glory to the newborn King." Charles Wesley, 1734

Prayer

Glory to God in the highest,
and peace to God's people on earth
Lord God, heavenly King,

Almighty God and Father we worship you,
we give you thanks, we praise you for your glory

Lord Jesus Christ, only Son of the Father,
Lord God, Lamb of God,
you take away the sins of the world;
have mercy on us;
you are seated at the right hand of the Father,
receive our prayer..

For you alone are the Holy One,

you alone are the Lord,
you alone are the Most High,
Jesus Christ,
with the Holy Spirit,
in the glory of God the Father.
Amen
Canticle of God's Glory

The Last Days

Scripture

38 "For I have come down from heaven .not to do My own will,
but the will of my Father who sent Me.
39"This is the will of Him who sent me that of all that He has
given Me, I will lose nothing, but raise it up on the last day.
40 For this is the will of My Father, that everyone who beholds the
Son and believes in Him will have eternal life, And I myself will
raise him up on the last day.
John 6: 38-40

23 This He said to her, "Your brother will rise again."
24 Martha said to Him, "I know that he will arise again in the
resurrection on the last day."
25 Jesus said to her, "I am the resurrection and the life; he who
believes in Me will live even if he dies.
26 and everyone who lives and believes in Me will never die. Do
you believe this?"
John 11: 23 - 26

3 As He was sitting on the Mount of Olives, the disciples came to
Him privately saying, "Tell us, when will these things happen, and
what will be the sign of Your coming, and of the end of the age?"
4 And Jesus answered them saying, "See to it that no one misleads
you.
5 "For many will come in My name, saying, "I am the Christ," and
will mislead many.
6 "You will be hearing of wars and rumors of wars. See that you
are not frightened, for those things must take place, but that is not
the end
7 "For nation will rise up against nation, and kingdom against
kingdom, for these things must take place,
But that is not yet the end.
8 "But all these things are merely the beginning of birth pains,
9 "Then they will deliver you to tribulation and will kill you, and
you will be hated by all nations because of My name.

10 At that time many will fall away and will betray one another and hate one another..

11 "Many false prophets will rise and will mislead many.

12 "Because lawlessness is increased, most peoples love will grow cold.

13 "But the one who endures to the end, he will be saved.

14 "The gospel of the kingdom shall be preached in the whole world as a testimony to all the nations, and then the end will come."

Matthew 24: 3 -14

35 "Heaven and earth will pass away, but my word will not pass away.

36 "But of the day or the hour no one knows, not even the angels of heaven, not the Son, but the Father
only.

37 "For the coming of the Son of man will be just like the days of Noah.

38 "For as the days before the flood they were eating and drinking, marrying and giving in marriage. Until Noah entered the ark.

39 and they did not understand until the flood came and took them all away; so will the coming of the
Son of man be.

40 "Then there will be two men in the field; one will be taken and the other will be left.

41 "Two women will be grinding at the mill; one will be taken and the other left..

42 "Therefore be on the alert, for you do not know which day the Lord is coming.

Matthew 24: 34 - 42

Meditation

Jesus said that the heavens and the earth will pass away but His word will never pass away. No one will know the day or the hour of the end of their lives on earth. Our heavenly Father is the only one who will know. Some of us will die suddenly of accidents, wars, heart attacks, homicide, or suicide, or other causes of instant death. Others will die slowly of illnesses, cancer or ageing. God's desire for us is to live a long and peaceful life and pass from this life to eternal life in peace. One of God's commandments was, "Honor your father and mother so that your days may be prolonged in the land which the Lord your God gives you." Exodus 20: 12

Jesus said that God's will is that everyone who believes in Him will not perish but have eternal life. When Martha told Jesus that if He had been there her brother would not have died. Jesus said to her, "I am the resurrection and the life; he who believes in Me will live even if he dies. John 11: 25 ,26

It was God's will for mankind to live a peaceful life and to have plenty when He placed man in the Garden of Eden, but man chose to gain all the knowledge he could, to control his own life and destiny. Few were those who chose to do God's will and leave their destiny to Him. As Jesus said, "Enter through the narrow gate, for the way is wide and the way is broad that leads to destruction, and there are many who will enter through it. For the gate is small and the way is narrow that leads to life, and there are few who find it. Matthew 2: 13, 14

Jesus told us that the earth would come to an end. God promised Noah that He would not destroy the earth by a flood of water again. Man will be eating and drinking and doing their usual things even in the last days.

We are having wars and rumors and rumors of wars every day now. Brother is fighting brother all over the world. Greed, pride, and lust has controlled many of man's lives. Some still walk the straight path and love, have faith, and live in fellowship and harmony with themselves and their neighbor. There is famine, earthquakes and floods in many places on the earth. Many are being persecuted and killed because of their beliefs. Man's love has grown cold.

Then God will judge between nations and shall rebuke many people and they will hammer their swords plowshares and their spears into pruning hooks. Nation will not lift up sword against nation and never again will war. Jesus said, "The gospel of the kingdom shall be preached as a testimony to all the nations, and then the end will come." Matthew 24: 24

Thoughts for the Week

One sweetly solemn thought comes to me o'er and o'er;
I am nearer home today than I ever been before.
Nearer my Father's house, where the many mansions be;
Nearer the great white throne, nearer the crystal sea.
Nearer the bounds of life where burdens are laid down.
Father, perfect my trust, strengthen the pow'r of faith;
Now let me stand, at last, alone on the shore of death.
Phoebe Cary

1 The Lord is my shepherd I shall not want.
2 He makes me lie down in green pastures;
3 He restores my soul; He guides me in the paths of righteousness For His names' sake.
4 Even though I walk through the valley of the shadow of death, I fear no evil, for You are with me;
Your rod and staff, they comfort me;
5 You prepare a table before me in the presence of my enemies; You have anointed my head with oil;
My cup overflows.
6Surely goodness and loving kindness will follow me all the days of my life. And I will dwell in the house of the Lord Forever. Psalm 23

Prayer

O day of God, draw nigh in beauty and in power,
Come with thy timeless judgment now to match our present hour.

Bring to our troubled minds, uncertain and afraid,
The quiet of a steadfast faith call of a call obeyed.

Bring to our world of strife and sovereign word of peace.
That war man haunts the earth no more, and desolation cease.

O day of God, draw nigh as at creation's birth;
let there be light again, and set thy judgment on the earth.
R. B. Y. Scott, 1937

Eternity

Scripture

10 "Blessed are those who are persecuted for the sake of righteousness, for theirs is the kingdom of heaven.
11 "Blessed are you when people insult you and persecute you and falsely say all kind of evil against you because of Me.
12 "Rejoice and be glad, for your reward in heave is great; for in the same way they persecuted the people who were before you.
Matthew 5: 10 -12

1 "Do not let your heart be troubled, believe in God; believe also in Me.
2 "In my Father's house are many dwelling places; if it were not so, I would have told you; for I go to a   place for you.
3 "If I go and prepare a place for you, I will come and receive you to Myself, that where I am there you may be also.
John 14: 1 - 3

31 "But when the Son of man comes in His glory and all and all the angels with Him, then He will sit on His glorious throne.
32 "All the nations will be gathered before Him; and He shall separate them one form another, as the shepherd separates the sheep from the goats;
33 and He will put the sheep on His right, and the goats on the left.
34 "Then the King will say to those on His right, "Come, you who are blessed of my Father, inherit the kingdom prepared for you from the foundation of the world.
Matthew 25:31 - 34

41 Then He will ay to those on his left, "Depart from Me you cured ones, into the eternal fire which has been for the devil and his angles;

42 for I was hungry and you gave Me nothing to eat, I was thirsty and you gave me nothing to drink;

43 I was a stranger and you did not invite me in, naked and you did not clothe Me; sick and in prison and you did not visit Me."
Matthew 25: 41 - 43

39 One of the criminals who were hanging there was hurling abuse at Him, "saying, are you not the Christ? save Yourself and us!

40 But the other answered, and rebuking him said, "Do you not even fear God, since you are under the same sentence of condemnation?

41 "And indeed we are suffering, for we are receiving what we deserve for our deeds; but this man has done nothing wrong."

42 And he was saying, "Jesus, remember me when You come in Your kingdom."

43 "And He said to him, "Truly I say to you, today you shall be with Me in Paradise."
Luke 23: 39 - 43

2 "In my Father's house are many dwelling places; if it were not so, I would have told you so; for I go to prepare a place for you.

3 "If I go and prepare a place for you, I will come again and receive you to Myself, that where I am, there you may be also.

4 "And you know the way where I am going."

5 Thomas said to Him, "Lord, we do not know where you are going, how we know the way?"

6 Jesus said to him, "I am the way, the truth, and the life; no one comes to the Father but through Me."

7 "If you have known Me, you have known my Father also; from now on you know Him and have seen Him."
John 14: 2 - 7

16 "I will ask the Father, and He will give you another
Helper, that He may be with you forever;
17 "that is the spirit of truth, whom the world cannot
because it does not see Him or Know Him, but you know
Him because he abides with you and will be in you.
18 "I will not leave you orphans; I will come to you
19 "After a little while the world will no longer see Me, but
you will see me; because I live, you will live also.
20 "In that day you will know that I am My Father, and you
in me, and I in you."
John 13: 16 – 20

Meditation

Our life on earth is a brief period compared to eternity, like
the twinkling of the eye. We are born to live only for a short
time. Then our earthly bodies are to become old and
destined to die. After we leave out bodies we are destined to
live an eternal life in the warmth of God's love.

Jesus, while teaching the people, described judgment day
and said, "But when the Son of man comes in His glory, and
all the angels with him, He will sit on His glorious throne.
All the nations gathered before Him; and He will separate
them from one another as the shepherd the sheep from the
goats; and He will put the sheep on His right, and the goats
on the left. Then the king will say to those on His right,
"Come, you who are blessed of My Father, inherit th
Kingdom prepared for you from the foundation of the world.
Matthew 25: 31 - 34

At the last supper with the disciples, Jesus was teaching them and said to them that He would be with them only a little while longer. They became concerned and that they did not know where He was going and what they would do. Jesus gave them a new commandment, that they should love one another, as He had loved them. By loving Hem and one another, all men know that they are His disciples; in they have love for each other.

Peter said, "Lord, where are you going?" Jesus answered, "Where I go, you cannot follow; but you will follow later." John 12: 36

Jesus said to His disciples, "If I go and prepare a place for you, I will come again and receive you to myself, that where I am, there you may be also and you know the way where I am going." Thomas said to Him, "Lord, we do not know where you are going, how we know the way?" Jesus said to Him, "I am the way, and the truth, and the life, no one comes to the Father but through me.   John 14: 5 – 10

Jesus said, "I will ask the Father, and He will give you another Helper, that He will be with you forever, that is the Spirit of truth, whom the world cannot receive, because it does not see him or know him, but you know Him because He abides with you and will be in you. I will not leave you as orphans; I will come to you. After a little while the world will not see Me; but you will see Me because I live, you will live also, In that day you will know that I an in My Father, and you in Me, and I in you.. John 14: 16 – 20

Man has difficulty understanding eternity. Man thinks mostly in the start and end of everything. Paul told us that we would not understand but see as looking in a mirror dimly. Now we know only in part, at for eternity we will know as we are known. There are numerous beliefs. Some believe that the only way to be with God for eternity is for the church leaders to present them to Jesus and for Jesus to present us to God. Some believe that you have to be baptized in a certain way. Others believe that you have to belong to a church with a certain name. Some believe that you have to die for the cause of their religion to go to heaven for eternity. Jesus never taught that there was a certain legal want to be with Him for eternity. He told the thief on the cross that he would be with Him in paradise, "this day." Jesus taught that we would with Him for eternity by the way we lived, loved and cared for others.

Thoughts for the Day

God sent His Son, they called Him Jesus;
he came to love, heal, and forgive;
he lived and died to buy my pardon,
an empty grave is there to prove that my Savior lives.

How sweet to hold a new born baby
and feel the pride and joy he gives;
but greater still the calm assurance,
this child can face uncertain days because he lives.

And one day I'll cross the river,
I'll fight life's final fight with pain
and as death gives way to victory,
I'll see the lights of glory and I'll know He reigns.
*Jesus
Gloria and William J. Gaither, 1971

Prayer

Lord, make me an instrument of thy peace;
Where there be hatred, let there be love;
Where there be injury, let there be pardon;
Where there be doubt, faith:
Where there be despair, hope;
Where there be darkness, light;
Where there be sadness, Joy.

O Divine Master, grant that I may not so much seek to be consoled
as to be consoled;
to be understood , as to understand;
to be loved, as to love;
for it is giving that we receive;
it is in pardon that we are pardoned;
and it is in dying that we are born to eternal life.
Amen
Frances of Assis, Italy, 14th century

www.ingramcontent.com/pod-product-compliance
Lightning Source LLC
LaVergne TN
LVHW051522080426
835509LV00017B/2175